STATISTICS DIRECTORATE

SERVICES
MEASURING
REAL ANNUAL VALUE ADDED

ORGANISATION FOR ECONOMIC CO-OPERATION AND DEVELOPMENT

ORGANISATION FOR ECONOMIC CO-OPERATION AND DEVELOPMENT

Pursuant to Article 1 of the Convention signed in Paris on 14th December 1960, and which came into force on 30th September 1961, the Organisation for Economic Co-operation and Development (OECD) shall promote policies designed:

- to achieve the highest sustainable economic growth and employment and a rising standard of living in Member countries, while maintaining financial stability, and thus to contribute to the development of the world economy;
- to contribute to sound economic expansion in Member as well as non-member countries in the process of economic development; and
- to contribute to the expansion of world trade on a multilateral, non-discriminatory basis in accordance with international obligations.

The original Member countries of the OECD are Austria, Belgium, Canada, Denmark, France, Germany, Greece, Iceland, Ireland, Italy, Luxembourg, the Netherlands, Norway, Portugal, Spain, Sweden, Switzerland, Turkey, the United Kingdom and the United States. The following countries became Members subsequently through accession at the dates indicated hereafter: Japan (28th April 1964), Finland (28th January 1969), Australia (7th June 1971), New Zealand (29th May 1973), Mexico (18th May 1994) and the Czech Republic (21st December 1995). The Commission of the European Communities takes part in the work of the OECD (Article 13 of the OECD Convention).

Publié en français sous le titre :

SERVICES

MESURE DE LA VALEUR AJOUTÉE RÉELLE ANNUELLE

TABLE OF CONTENTS

Page

INTRODUCTION

Between the sixties and the nineties the share of services, market and non-market, has climbed from one half to two thirds of Gross Domestic Product (GDP) in the OECD area. The quality of measures of service value added at constant prices is, therefore, not only important per se but also essential to derive reliable statistics on the growth of GDP and on national productivity trends.

The purpose of this publication is to contribute towards improving and standardising data on value added in service activities. In 1987, the OECD published a report[1] on methods used by Member countries to estimate value added at constant prices in service activities within the National Accounts framework. Since then, most Member countries have worked to improve their estimates of the price/volume breakdown of services and have implemented a number of changes in estimation methods[2]. For these reasons an updated and enlarged study on national practices was considered appropriate and timely.

The service activities covered in this study are those included in categories G to P of the International Industrial Classification of all Economic Activities, Revision 3, hereafter referred to as ISIC[3]. These cover:

G   Wholesale and retail trade; repair of motor vehicles, motor-cycles and personal and household goods; retail sale of automotive fuel
H   Hotels and restaurants
I   Transport, storage and communications
J   Financial intermediation
K   Real estate, renting and business services
L   Public administration and defence; compulsory social security
M   Education
N   Health and social work
O   Other community, social and personal service activities
P   Private households with employed persons.

---

1) OECD (1987), *Measurement of Value Added at Constant Prices in Service Activities, Sources and Methods*, Paris.

2) The U.S. provide an example of recent improvement in methods and source data collection [cf. De Leeuw F., M. Mohr and R.P. Parker, *Gross Product by Industry, 1977-1988, A Progress Report on Improving the Estimates*, U.S. Department of Commerce, Survey of Current Business, January 1991].

3) United Nations (1990), *International Standard Industrial Classification of All Economic Activities*, Series M. No. 4, Rev. 3, New York.

Chapter 1 provides an overview of the various methods in use; Chapter 2 classifies countries according to the types of methods mainly used; Chapter 3 shows, in tabular form, the methods used for each service category with an annex table showing the quantitative importance of each method; Chapter 4 provides a detailed description of the various deflators and extrapolators used by Member countries for each service category.

The information contained in this report was obtained from a questionnaire sent to national statistical offices in all Member countries. The study describes the methods and indices used to produce annual estimates of constant price value added as of June 1995. The Secretariat is grateful to national experts for their help in completing the questionnaire, in providing additional information on request and in reviewing earlier drafts of this report.

CHAPTER 1: **OVERVIEW OF METHODS**

A large variety of different methods have been devised by countries to estimate the real value added of service activities. In this report, the different methods have been categorised by cross-classifying the following elements:

a) the use of double or single indicator methods,

b) the use of output- or input-related indicators,

c) the use of deflation or extrapolation,

d) the type of variable on which the indicators are based.

Thirteen principle methods have been distinguished and a fourteenth category covers all other method. The methods are described in the following paragraphs and a general formula is given for each one of them. This classification draws heavily on that used in the 1971 study by T.P Hill[4].

Double indicator methods take into account changes in both outputs and inputs of goods and services, and value added is derived as a residual by subtracting constant price estimates of intermediate consumption from constant price estimates of gross output. Single indicator methods consist in estimating constant price value added using a single variable, the movements of which are assumed to be correlated with those of value added. Double indicator methods are, from a theoretical standpoint, superior to single indicator methods, since they take into account changes of both outputs and inputs and derive value added as a residual, in conformity with its definition.

Three types of double indicator methods are identified according to whether price or quantity indices are used. For quantity indices a distinction is made between volumes and physical quantities; the former are expressed in deflated monetary units, the latter in physical units such as tonnes, kilometres, numbers of persons employed, number of medical consultations, etc.

A. DOUBLE INDICATOR METHODS

a) **Double deflation**: in double deflation, current price series of gross output and of intermediate consumption are both deflated by price indices which measure the change in prices of output on the one hand and of inputs of goods and services on the other. This method is considered preferable to others from a conceptual point of view because not only is constant price value added obtained as a residual, but also because price relatives tend to be more stable over time than corresponding quantity relatives. The former can take into account new products as they appear on the market and progressively eliminate obsolete ones as they disappear without creating breaks in time series. Quantity relatives, on the other hand may take on extreme values varying between infinity and zero as new commodities are offered on markets and old ones disappear, thus causing erratic movements in value added.

---

4)   Hill T.P. (1971), *The measurement of Real Product; a theoretical and empirical analysis of the growth rates for different industries and countries*, OECD, Paris.

The general method may be formulated as follows:

$$VAR_t = \frac{Y_t}{IPY_t} - \frac{C_t}{IPC_t}$$

where:

VAR_t represents constant price value added in year t

Y_t represents current price gross output in year t

IPY_t represents a price index of gross output in year t

C_t represents current price intermediate consumption in year t

IPC_t represents a price index of intermediate consumption in year t

b)   **Double extrapolation**: in double extrapolation, base year values of gross output and of intermediate consumption are extrapolated using volume or physical quantity indices, and derive constant price value added by subtraction. This method presents the advantage of taking into account both elements which are used to define value added. On the other hand, it presents the disadvantage that quality changes are not easily taken into account, particularly when physical quantity indices are used.

The general method can be formulated as follows, if a volume index is used as extrapolator:

$$VAR_t = Y_0 \times IVY_t - C_0 \times IVC_t$$

or as follows, if a physical quantity output index is used as extrapolator:

$$VAR_t = Y_0 \times IQY_t - C_0 \times IQC_t$$

where:

VAR_t represents constant price value added in year t

Y_0 represents base year gross output

IVY_t represents a volume index of gross output in year t

C_0 represents base year intermediate consumption

IVC_t represents a volume index of intermediate consumption in year t

IQY_t represents a physical quantity output index in year t

IQC_t represents a physical quantity index of intermediate consumption in year t

c) **Extrapolation / deflation** consists in deriving constant price value added from an extrapolated series of base year estimates of gross output, using output volume or physical quantity indices and a deflated series of current price intermediate consumption using price indices (or vice versa, though this is more rarely the case).

The method may be formulated as follows if volume indices are used as extrapolators:

$$VAR_t = Y_0 \times IVY_t - \frac{C_t}{IPC_t} \qquad \text{or alternatively} \qquad \frac{Y_t}{IPY_t} - C_0 \times IVC_t$$

or, as follows if physical quantity indices are used as extrapolators:

$$VAR_t = Y_0 \times IQY_t - \frac{C_t}{IPC_t} \qquad \text{or alternatively} \qquad \frac{Y_t}{IPY_t} - C_0 \times IQC_t$$

where:

VAR_t represents constant price value added in year t

Y_0 represents base year gross output

IVY_t represents the volume index of gross output in year t

C_t represents current price intermediate consumption in year t

IPC_t represents the price index for intermediate consumption in year t

Y_t represents current price gross output in year t

IPY_t represents a price index of gross output in year t

C_0 represents base year intermediate consumption

IVC_t represents a volume index of intermediate consumption in year t

IQY_t represents a physical quantity output index in year t

IQC_t represents a physical quantity intermediate consumption index in year t

B.   SINGLE INDICATOR METHODS

Single indicator methods are classified according to whether the indicator is output- or input-related, according to whether deflation or extrapolation is used and according to the variable chosen as a proxy for measuring volume changes in value added.

Single output-related indicator methods are classified into three variants:

a) **Direct deflation** of current price value added by a gross output price index, a consumer price index, or its relevant components.

This method may be formulated as follows:

$$VAR_t = \frac{VAC_t}{IPY_t} \qquad \text{or} \qquad VAR_t = \frac{VAC_t}{CPI_t}$$

where:

VAR_t represents constant price value added in year t

VAC_t represents current price value added in year t

IPY_t represents the gross output price index in year t

CPI_t represents the consumer price index or its relevant components in year t

The producer price index is generally preferred to the consumer price index. Yet when there are no intermediaries between the producer and consumer of a service, the consumer price index, or even better its relevant components, may be taken as a good proxy for the producer price index.

b)   **Direct extrapolation** of base year value added using a gross output volume index. The latter may be obtained by deflating current price gross output by an output price index or by extrapolating base year gross output by an output volume index.

This method may be formulated as follows:

$$VAR_t = VA_0 \times IVY_t \quad \text{with} \quad IVY_t = \frac{Y_t}{IPY_t} \qquad \text{or alternatively} \qquad IVY_t = Y_0 \times IVY_t$$

where:

VAR_t represents constant price value added in year t

VA_0 represents base year value added

IVY_t represents the gross output volume index in year t

Y_t represents current price gross output in year t

IPY_t represents the gross output price index in year t

Y_0 represents base year gross output

c)   **Direct extrapolation** of base year value added using indices based on physical quantity output measures. This approach differs from b) in that the basic data used to construct the extrapolator are expressed in physical units of output and not in deflated monetary units.

This method may be formulated as follows:

$$VAR_t = VA_0 \times IQY_t$$

where:

VAR_t represents constant price value added in year t

VA_0 represents base year value added

IQY_t represents a physical quantity output index in year t

Single input-related indicator methods are classified into nine categories according to whether deflation or extrapolation is used and according to which variable is taken as a proxy indicator for volume changes in value added.

a) **Direct deflation** of current price value added by a price index of intermediate consumption.

This method may be formulated as follows:

$$VAR_t = \frac{VAC_t}{IPC_t}$$

where:

VAR_t represents constant price value added in year t

VAC_t represents current price value added in year t

IPC_t represents an intermediate consumption price index in year t

b) **Direct deflation** of current price value added by a wage rate index.

This method may be formulated as follows:

$$VAR_t = \frac{VAC_t}{IW_t}$$

where:

VAR_t represents constant price value added in year t

VAC_t represents current price value added in year t

IW_t represents a nominal wage rate index in year t

c) **Direct extrapolation** of base year value added by a volume index of intermediate consumption.

This method may be formulated as follows:

$$VAR_t = VA_0 \times IVC_t$$

11

where:

VAR_t represents constant price value added in year t

VA_0 represents base year value added

IVC_t represents a volume index of intermediate consumption in year t

d) **Direct extrapolation** of base year value added using an index of deflated compensation of employees by a wage rate index.

This method may be formulated as follows:

$$VAR_t = VA_0 \times \frac{SAL_t}{IW_t}$$

where:

VAR_t represents constant price value added in year t

VA_0 represents base year value added

SAL_t represents compensation of employees in year t

IW_t represents a wage rate index in year t

e) **Direct extrapolation** of base year value added by an index based on physical quantities of inputs other than labour.

This method may be formulated as follows:

$$VAR_t = VA_0 \times IQC_t$$

where:

VAR_t represents constant price value added in year t

VA_0 represents base year value added

IQC_t represents a physical quantity index of inputs other than labour in year t

f) **Direct extrapolation** of base year value added by an index of numbers employed.

This method may be formulated as follows:

$$VAR_t = VA_0 \times IN_t$$

where:

VAR_t represents constant price value added in year t

VA_0 represents base year value added

IN_t represents an index of numbers employed in year t

g)   **Direct extrapolation** of base year value added by an index of man-hours worked.

This method may be formulated as follows:

$$VAR_t = VA_0 \times IH_t$$

where:

VAR_t represents constant price value added in year t

VA_0 represents base year value added

IH_t represents an index of hours worked in year t

h*) **Direct extrapolation** of base year value added by an index of hours or man-hours worked adjusted for change in labour productivity.

This method may be formulated as follows:

$$VAR_t = VA_0 \times IH^*_t$$

where:

VAR_t represents constant price value added in year t

VA_0 represents base year value added

IH^*_t represents an index of hours worked in year t adjusted for labour productivity change

i)   **Other method** includes estimation methods of constant price value added which do not fall into any of the above categories. For instance, the measurement of constant price value added may combine output and input indicators (e.g. the number of pupils and the number of teachers for educational services). Another example is the use of data relative to a different service activity than the one being measured, but closely related to it, for lack of any data on the latter (e.g. data on transport activities may serve as a proxy indicator for storage when no information on storage is available). A third example is the use of data on constant price private consumption for those industries which primarily serve consumers.

CHAPTER 2: **OVERVIEW OF COUNTRY PRACTICES**

As shown in Chapter 1, methods and indices differ considerably between countries and service categories. Despite this, an approximate classification of countries can be done by making a distinction between those which exclusively (or mainly) apply double indicator methods and those for which single indicator methods are predominantly used.

A. Use of double indicator methods

Japan and **Denmark** use double deflation for all service activities, both market and non-market. **Italy** uses double deflation for all market services and for non-market services produced by private households with employed persons. For government-produced non-market services, extrapolation/deflation is used and extrapolation of base year value added is used for activities of membership organisations. **Norway** applies double indicator methods throughout the service sector. Gross output is alternatively deflated or extrapolated. For a small number of services, components of gross output are partly deflated and partly extrapolated. This is the case for financial intermediation and for market human health activities. There is one exception - households with employed persons - where value added is deflated directly.

The **United States** uses double deflation for a majority of service activities. Extrapolation/deflation is used for transport activities except for water transport and activities auxiliary to transport. Extrapolation of base year value added is applied to water transport and supporting and auxiliary transport activities, to post and courier activities, financial intermediation, most business services, government operated non-market services (except health) and non-government/non-profit research and development activities. Direct deflation of current price value added is applied to real estate activities including owner-occupied and rented dwellings, to accounting, book-keeping, auditing and tax consultancy, business and management consultancy, research, architectural, engineering and other technical activities, to motion picture and video production, distribution and projection, library, archives, museums and other cultural activities, government operated health services and research and development and social work activities and private households with employed persons.

Germany uses double deflation for all market services except trade where value added is extrapolated directly. Direct deflation of value added is applied to non-market services. The few exceptions relate to activities of membership associations, non-profit institutions and private households with employed persons where base year value added is extrapolated. **France** uses double deflation for all market services except trade and transport activities for which extrapolation/deflation is used; direct deflation of current price value added is applied to non-market services, except for education where base year value added is extrapolated.

Canada uses double deflation for market services except for some sub-items of transport (other land freight transport, inland water transport, some supporting and auxiliary transport activities, transport via pipelines) and for national post and most of telecommunications to which extrapolation/deflation is applied. For most non-market services, a method using partly extrapolation and partly deflation is applied to the components of value added. Exceptions are defence activities, parts of regulation and contribution to more efficient operation of business, dramatic arts, music and other arts activities, sporting and other recreational activities, medical and dental practice activities, social work activities, activities of membership organisations n.e.c. and private households with employed persons; for these services current price value added is deflated directly. The **Netherlands** uses double deflation for a majority of market services. Exceptions are computer and related activities, research and development, other business services (except legal activities), news agency activities, part of human health activities, sewage and refuse disposal where current price value added is deflated directly. Extrapolation of base year value added is used for recreational and cultural activities (except radio and television) and for financial intermediation. For all non-market services value added is deflated directly.

Sweden applies double deflation to market services whenever complete data on gross output and on intermediate consumption are available. This is the case for rail, sea and air transport and for post and telecommunications. For other market services, for which complete data on intermediate consumption are not available, a "special" double indicator approach is used which may be called "controlled double deflation or extrapolation/deflation". This method is described under "Other methods" in Chapter 3. Two exceptions to the use of double indicator methods for market services are financial intermediation where base year value added is extrapolated, and activities of membership organisations (excluding activities of business, employers and professional organisations) where value added is deflated.

The information provided by the **United States**, **Japan**, **Germany**, **Canada**, **Denmark**, the **Netherlands** and **Norway** on how they obtain constant price estimates of inputs shows that these are calculated within the framework of input-output tables. Although there are variations between countries at the detailed level, the overall approach to deflation of inputs of goods and services is comparable. Inputs are deflated at a detailed level and a distinction is made between domestically produced and imported commodities. Prices used for deflation of domestically produced inputs are derived from the producer price index, the consumer price index or an implicit price index. Prices of imports are also taken from a variety of sources. The weights for prices are derived from the input composition of the base year input-output table, on the assumption that the input structure remains unchanged in constant prices. This leads to the calculation of an implicit deflator for the total intermediate consumption of a given industry. There are exceptions to this method when the information on the composition of inputs for an industry is unreliable, or has changed significantly since the benchmark year. Countries then resort to a variety of proxy methods in order to obtain an alternative implicit deflator for inputs.

B. Use of single indicator methods

The **United Kingdom**, **Iceland**, **Ireland**, **Portugal**, **Switzerland**, **Turkey**, **Australia** and **New Zealand** use exclusively single indicator methods. For market services, the **United Kingdom** uses mainly extrapolation of base year value added except for the sale, maintenance and repair of motor vehicles and motor-cycles, hotels and restaurants and life insurance where current price value added is deflated. Value added for non-market services is extrapolated. **Iceland** deflates current price value added for market services except for financial intermediation and health services where base year value added is extrapolated, and applies a mixture of direct deflation and extrapolation of value added for computer and related activities, business and management consultancy, architectural, engineering and other technical activities, advertising, business activities n.e.c., human health activities, radio and television activities, other entertainment activities n.e.c., sporting and other entertainment activities and other service activities. Base year value added for veterinary services and for non-market services is extrapolated.

Ireland extrapolates base year value added for market and non-market services with the exception of state-owned rented dwellings, where current price value added is deflated. **Portugal** uses direct deflation of current price value added for supporting and auxiliary transport activities; activities of travel agencies, monetary and other financial intermediation, renting of transport equipment and of other machinery and equipment. Value added for transport activities and post and telecommunication is extrapolated. A mixed method using partly direct deflation and partly direct extrapolation is applied to wholesale and retail trade. For non-market services direct deflation is used except for education and recreational, cultural and sporting activities to which direct extrapolation is applied. **Switzerland** applies direct extrapolation to base year value added for both market and non-market services. **Turkey** applies direct deflation to current price value added of market services except to financial intermediation where base year value added is extrapolated. **Australia** derives constant price value added by direct extrapolation of both market and non-market services. **New Zealand** uses direct extrapolation of base year value added for market services except for other land transport, part of sea transport of freight and supporting and auxiliary air transport activities where current price value added is deflated. Value added for non-market services is obtained by direct extrapolation except for activities performed by non-government non-profit institutions known as QUANGOS for which value added is obtained by direct deflation.

Austria uses single indicator methods for most market services. Direct deflation of current price value added is used more or less as frequently as extrapolation of base year value added. Two exceptions concern post and telecommunications and owner-occupied or rented dwellings where double deflation is applied. Single indicator methods are applied to non-market services, either direct deflation or extrapolation. **Belgium** uses direct deflation of value added for market services except for wholesale and retail trade, rail and inland water transport, supporting and auxiliary services to transport, owner-occupied and rented dwellings, part of human health activities (excluding hospitals) where extrapolation of base year value added is used. Double deflation is used for sea transport, double extrapolation for air transport and partly double extrapolation, partly extrapolation to sale, maintenance and repair of motor vehicles and motor-cycles. Direct deflation of value added is applied to non-market services.

Finland uses both direct deflation and extrapolation of value added. Exceptions to the use of these methods concern wholesale and retail trade (including repair of motor vehicles, motor-cycles and personal and household goods), hotels and restaurants, financial intermediation, human health activities, sewage and refuse disposal and radio and television activities: for these activities, double deflation is used. Extrapolation/deflation is applied to owner-occupied and rented dwellings and adult and other education,. Value added of non-market services is deflated directly. **Luxembourg** extrapolates value added of market services except for financial intermediation to which extrapolation/deflation is applied and other financial services for which direct extrapolation is used. Value added for non-market services is obtained through extrapolation of base year value added. **Spain** mainly uses extrapolation of base year value added, but various other methods are also used. Deflation of current price value added is applied to supporting and auxiliary transport activities, financial intermediation and adult and other education. Double deflation is used for transport by rail, real estate activities, advertising, health services, recreational, cultural and sporting activities. Extrapolation/deflation is applied to other land passenger and to air transport. A mixture of double deflation and direct deflation is used for post and telecommunications . Constant price value added of non-market services is obtained partly by extrapolation and partly by deflation.

Productivity Change

Several countries adjust indices to take into account labour productivity change; the **United Kingdom**, for financial intermediation, research and development, other business services, market research and public opinion polling, business and management consultancy, architectural, engineering and other technical activities, advertising and various business services n.e.c., education and human health market services, sewage and refuse disposal and other service activities; **Germany** for government operated non-market services; **Austria** for computer and related activities, research and development, other business activities and veterinary activities; **Luxembourg** for all non-market services except private households with employed persons (+ 0.5% per year); the **Netherlands** for computer and related activities, market research and development, market sewage and refuse disposal, sanitation and similar activities, public administration and defence, non-market education, research and development and private households with employed persons; **Sweden** for financial intermediation(+ 2% per year).

CHAPTER 3 - **METHODS USED**

This chapter identifies the methods used by countries to measure constant price value added for the activities covered in categories G to P of the ISIC listed in the introduction. These categories are broken down to identify detailed services activities.

It should be noted that the classifications used by countries do not correspond exactly to the ISIC and countries have been assigned to the ISIC groups which most closely approximate the groups used in their national classifications. It should also be noted that when countries report that they use a particular method to derive constant price estimates for a group of activities taken together (e.g. all rail transport services), they are listed in the appropriate column for each of the sub-components (e.g. passenger transport and freight transport), even though they may not compile or publish estimates at this level of detail.

A distinction is made in the table between market services and non-market services. The latter are mainly provided by general government in areas such as public administration, defence, public order, health and education, but they also include the services of private non-profit institutions serving households and the services provided by private households with employed persons (i.e. with domestic staff).

In this chapter, countries are identified by the following abbreviations:

ABBREVIATION	COUNTRY	ABBREVIATION	COUNTRY
US	United States	IR	Ireland
JA	Japan	LU	Luxembourg
GE	Germany	NE	Netherlands
FR	France	NO	Norway
UK	United Kingdom	PO	Portugal
IT	Italy	SP	Spain
CA	Canada	SE	Sweden
AU	Austria	SW	Switzerland
BE	Belgium	TU	Turkey
DE	Denmark	AL	Australia
FI	Finland	NZ	New Zealand
IC	Iceland		

Annex 3.1 at the end of this chapter shows, for each country, the shares in total service value added obtained by the different methods.

MEASUREMENT METHODS OF VALUE ADDED AT CONSTANT PRICES IN SERVICE ACTIVITIES

ISIC Revision 3	Double Indicators			Single indicators		
				Output related indices		
	Double deflation	Double extrapolation	Extrapolation /deflation	Deflated value added	Extrapolated value added	
					Volume	Physical quantity
A. MARKET SERVICES						
50 Sale, maintenance and repair of motor vehicles and motorcycles (including parts, accessories and fuel)	US JA FR IT DE (1) FI NE NO		SE (5)	UK AU IC	GE LU SP NZ	AL
51 Wholesale trade (except of motor vehicles and motorcycles)	US JA IT CA DE FI NE NO		FR	AU IC PO	GE UK (6) LU SP SW (7) AL NZ	UK NZ (8)
52 Retail trade (except of motor vehicles and motorcycles, including repair of personal and household goods)	US (2) JA IT CA DE (3) FI NE NO SE (4)		FR	AU IC PO	GE UK LU SP SW (7) AL NZ	

NOTES

1. DE Excludes sales of motor vehicles.
2. US Includes restaurants, bars and canteens.
3. DE Includes sales of motor vehicles.
4. SE Repair of personal and household goods.
5. SE Repair of motor vehicles.

MEASUREMENT METHODS OF VALUE ADDED AT CONSTANT PRICES IN SERVICE ACTIVITIES

Single indicators							Other Methods
Input related indices							
Deflated value added		Extrapolated value added					
Intermediate consumption price	Wage rate	Intermediate consumption volume	Deflated wage bill	Input physical quantity	Numbers employed	Hours worked	
							BE IR SE (9) TU
					PO		BE IR SE TU
					PO		IR SE TU

6. UK Only food and drink.
7. SW Includes motor vehicles.
8. NZ Petroleum products.
9. SE Excludes repair of motor vehicles.

MEASUREMENT METHODS OF VALUE ADDED AT CONSTANT PRICES IN SERVICE ACTIVITIES

ISIC Revision 3	Double Indicators			Single indicators		
				Output related indices		
	Double deflation	Double extrapolation	Extrapolation /deflation	Deflated value added	Extrapolated value added	
					Volume	Physical quantity
551 Hotels, camping sites and other short stay accommodation	US JA GE FR IT CA DE FI NE NO SE			UK AU BE IC TU	LU NZ	AU (3) SP SW AL
552 Restaurants, bars and canteens	JA GE FR IT CA DE FI NE NO (1) SE		NO (2)	UK AU BE IC TU	LU AL NZ	SW
601 Transport via railways - passengers	JA GE IT CA DE NE NO SP SE		US FR	FI TU	AL NZ	UK AU BE FI IR LU PO SW

NOTES

1. NO Excluding drinks.
2. NO Drinks only.
3. AU Lodging in private homes.
4. IR Excludes public houses which are classified in retail trade.

MEASUREMENT METHODS OF VALUE ADDED AT CONSTANT PRICES IN SERVICE ACTIVITIES

Single indicators							Other Methods
Input related indices							
Deflated value added		Extrapolated value added					
Intermediate consumption price	Wage rate	Intermediate consumption volume	Deflated wage bill	Input physical quantity	Numbers employed	Hours worked	
							IR
				SP IR (4)			

MEASUREMENT METHODS OF VALUE ADDED AT CONSTANT PRICES IN SERVICE ACTIVITIES

ISIC Revision 3	Double Indicators			Single indicators		
					Output related indices	
	Double deflation	Double extrapolation	Extrapolation /deflation	Deflated value added	Extrapolated value added	
					Volume	Physical quantity
- freight	JA GE IT CA DE NE SP	NO	US FR SE	FI TU		UK AU BE FI IR LU PO SW AL NZ
602 Other land transport						
- passengers	JA GE IT CA DE NE SE (1)		US FR NO SP SE (2)	AU FI (3) IC TU NZ	UK (4) LU AL	UK (5) BE FI (6) IR (7) PO SW AL
- freight	JA GE IT DE NE SE	NO	US FR CA	AU IC NZ	LU	UK BE FI (8) IR SP SW AL
603 Transport via pipelines	GE IT NE	NO	US FR CA	TU	FI	BE AU

NOTES

1. SE Bus transport.
2. SE Taxis.
3. FI   Bus transport.
4. UK Taxis.
5. UK Bus transport.

MEASUREMENT METHODS OF VALUE ADDED AT CONSTANT PRICES IN SERVICE ACTIVITIES

Single indicators							Other Methods
Input related indices							
Deflated value added		Extrapolated value added					
Intermediate consumption price	Wage rate	Intermediate consumption volume	Deflated wage bill	Input physical quantity	Numbers employed	Hours worked	
				IR (9)	FI (6)		
				FI (10)			TU
							AL

6. FI   Taxis.
7. IR   Bus transport.
8. FI   Scheduled transport.
9. IR   Taxis.
10. FI   Mainly charter transport.

MEASUREMENT METHODS OF VALUE ADDED AT CONSTANT PRICES IN SERVICE ACTIVITIES

ISIC Revision 3	Double Indicators			Single indicators		
					Output related indices	
	Double deflation	Double extrapolation	Extrapolation /deflation	Deflated value added	Extrapolated value added	
					Volume	Physical quantity
611 Sea transport						
- passengers	JA GE IT CA BE DE NE NO		FR SE	FI IC TU	UK	AU IR PO SP SW AL NZ
- freight	JA GE IT CA BE DE NE NO SE		FR	FI IC NZ (1)	UK AL	AU IR PO SP SW AL NZ (1)
612 Inland water transport						
- passengers	JA GE CA DE NE NO SE		FR	FI		UK AU BE LU AL
- freight	JA GE CA DE NE NO SE		FR	FI		UK AU BE LU AL

NOTES

1. NZ Different methods used for different operators.

MEASUREMENT METHODS OF VALUE ADDED AT CONSTANT PRICES IN SERVICE ACTIVITIES

Single indicators							Other Methods
Input related indices							
Deflated value added		Extrapolated value added					
Intermediate consumption price	Wage rate	Intermediate consumption volume	Deflated wage bill	Input physical quantity	Numbers employed	Hours worked	
					US		
					US		TU
					US		
					US		

MEASUREMENT METHODS OF VALUE ADDED AT CONSTANT PRICES IN SERVICE ACTIVITIES

ISIC Revision 3	Double Indicators			Single indicators		
				Output related indices		
	Double deflation	Double extrapolation	Extrapolation /deflation	Deflated value added	Extrapolated value added	
					Volume	Physical quantity
62 Air transport						
- passengers	JA GE IT CA DE NE NO SE	BE	US FR SP	IC TU	IR (3)	UK AU FI IR (4) LU PO SW AL NZ
- freight	JA GE IT CA DE NE NO	BE	US FR SE SP	FI (1) IC TU		UK AU FI IR LU PO SW AL NZ
63 Supporting and auxiliary transport activities ; activities of travel agencies	JA GE FR IT CA DE NE		NO SE	AU FI IC SP NZ (2)	UK LU	BE LU NZ (2)

NOTES

1. FI Only stevedoring.
2. NZ Different methods are used for different operators.
3. IR State owned air transport.
4. IR Privately owned air transport.

MEASUREMENT METHODS OF VALUE ADDED AT CONSTANT PRICES IN SERVICE ACTIVITIES

Single indicators							Other Methods
Input related indices							
Deflated value added		Extrapolated value added					
Intermediate consumption price	Wage rate	Intermediate consumption volume	Deflated wage bill	Input physical quantity	Numbers employed	Hours worked	
					US		IR AL

MEASUREMENT METHODS OF VALUE ADDED AT CONSTANT PRICES IN SERVICE ACTIVITIES

ISIC Revision 3	Double Indicators			Single indicators		
					Output related indices	
	Double deflation	Double extrapolation	Extrapolation /deflation	Deflated value added	Extrapolated value added	
					Volume	Physical quantity
64 Post and Telecommunications	GE IT AU NE SE		FR	IC TU	SW	
641 Post and courier activities	JA GE DE NO SP (1) SE		FR CA	BE	FI SP (1) AL	US UK IR (6) LU PO AL NZ
642 Telecommunications	US JA GE CA (2) DE NO SP (1) SE		FR CA (3)	BE (4) FI	UK SP (1) AL NZ (5)	IR LU PO AL NZ (7)
651 Monetary intermediation	JA GE FR IT CA DE FI		LU NO	BE SP PO	UK AU IR SW NZ	UK

* Identifies indicators adjusted for labour productivity change.

NOTES

1. SP   Uses double deflation or extrapolation depending on available data.
2. CA   Cable TV only.
3. CA   Includes most of telecommunications.
4. BE   Telephone and telegraph.
5. NZ   Domestic trafic.

MEASUREMENT METHODS OF VALUE ADDED AT CONSTANT PRICES IN SERVICE ACTIVITIES

Single indicators							Other Methods
Input related indices							
Deflated value added		Extrapolated value added					
Intermediate consumption price	Wage rate	Intermediate consumption volume	Deflated wage bill	Input physical quantity	Numbers employed	Hours worked	
					IR (9)		
BE (8)						NZ (10)	
		NE	IC NE		US UK* IC TU	SE* AL	

6. IR State enterprises.
7. NZ International trafic.
8. BE Radio and television broadcasting.
9. IR Private sector.
10. NZ Applies to own account capital formation.

ISIC Revision 3		Double Indicators			Single indicators		
						Output related indices	
		Double deflation	Double extrapolation	Extrapolation /deflation	Deflated value added	Extrapolated value added	
						Volume	Physical quantity
659	Other financial intermediation	JA GE FR IT CA DE FI		NO	BE SP PO	UK AU IR LU NZ (3)	UK
6601	Life insurance	US JA GE FR IT CA DE FI		NO	UK BE SP	IR SW NZ	AU IR LU
6602- 6603	Other insurance (except compulsory social security)	JA GE FR IT CA DE FI		NO	AU BE SP	UK IR SW NZ	LU
67	Activities auxiliary to financial intermediation	US (1) JA GE FR CA		US (2)	AU BE	UK LU NZ	UK

* Identifies indicators adjusted for labour productivity change.

NOTES

1. US Mutual fund sales, underwriting and security exchanges.
2. US Commissions of security brokers and dealers.
3. NZ   Excludes the Reserve Bank.
4. NZ   Reserve Bank.
5. US Holding and other investment companies.

MEASUREMENT METHODS OF VALUE ADDED AT CONSTANT PRICES IN SERVICE ACTIVITIES

Single indicators							Other Methods
Input related indices							
Deflated value added		Extrapolated value added					
Intermediate consumption price	Wage rate	Intermediate consumption volume	Deflated wage bill	Input physical quantity	Numbers employed	Hours worked	
		NE	IC NE		US UK IC NZ (4) TU	SE* AL	
		NE	IC NE		IC TU	SE* AL	
		NE	IC NE		IC TU	SE* AL	
		NE	IC NE		US (5) IC TU	SE* AL	IR

33

MEASUREMENT METHODS OF VALUE ADDED AT CONSTANT PRICES IN SERVICE ACTIVITIES

ISIC Revision 3	Double Indicators			Single indicators		
				Output related indices		
	Double deflation	Double extrapolation	Extrapolation /deflation	Deflated value added	Extrapolated value added	
					Volume	Physical quantity
70 Real estate activities						
Owner-occupied dwellings	US GE FR IT CA AU DE NE NO SP		FI SE	US TU	UK IC IR LU AL	NZ
Rented dwellings	US JA GE FR IT AU DE NE NO SP		FI SE	US IR (1) TU	UK IR (2) LU AL NZ (3)	NZ (4)
Other real estate activities	JA GE FR IT DE NE NO SP		FI SE	US BE AU IC	UK LU	NZ

NOTES

1. IR   State housing.
2. IR   Private housing.
3. NZ   Commercial property rentals.
4. NZ   Residential property rentals.

MEASUREMENT METHODS OF VALUE ADDED AT CONSTANT PRICES IN SERVICE ACTIVITIES

Single indicators							Other Methods
Input related indices							
Deflated value added		Extrapolated value added					
Intermediate consumption price	Wage rate	Intermediate consumption volume	Deflated wage bill	Input physical quantity	Numbers employed	Hours worked	
			SW				BE
			SW				BE
					UK AL		UK IR TU

MEASUREMENT METHODS OF VALUE ADDED AT CONSTANT PRICES IN SERVICE ACTIVITIES

ISIC Revision 3	Double Indicators			Single indicators		
				Output related indices		
	Double deflation	Double extrapolation	Extrapolation /deflation	Deflated value added	Extrapolated value added	
					Volume	Physical quantity
711 Renting of transport equipment	US JA GE FR IT CA FI NE NO		SE	BE IC PO	UK LU	AU
712 Renting of other machinery and equipment	JA GE FR IT CA DE FI NE NO SE			BE IC PO	UK LU	AU
713 Renting of personal and household goods	JA GE FR IT CA FI NE NO SE			BE IC	UK AU LU	

MEASUREMENT METHODS OF VALUE ADDED AT CONSTANT PRICES IN SERVICE ACTIVITIES

Single indicators							Other Methods
Input related indices							
Deflated value added		Extrapolated value added					
Intermediate consumption price	Wage rate	Intermediate consumption volume	Deflated wage bill	Input physical quantity	Numbers employed	Hours worked	
					SP NZ	AL NZ	IR
					SP NZ	AL NZ	IR

MEASUREMENT METHODS OF VALUE ADDED AT CONSTANT PRICES IN SERVICE ACTIVITIES

ISIC Revision 3	Double Indicators			Single indicators		
				Output related indices		
	Double deflation	Double extrapolation	Extrapolation /deflation	Deflated value added	Extrapolated value added	
					Volume	Physical quantity
72 Computer and related activities	JA GE FR IT CA DE FI NO SE			BE IC	UK LU	
73 Research and development	JA GE FR IT CA FI		SE	BE	LU	
74 Other business services	JA GE FR IT SE			BE	LU	

* Identifies indicators adjusted for labour productivity change.

MEASUREMENT METHODS OF VALUE ADDED AT CONSTANT PRICES IN SERVICE ACTIVITIES

Single indicators							Other Methods
Input related indices							
Deflated value added		Extrapolated value added					
Intermediate consumption price	Wage rate	Intermediate consumption volume	Deflated wage bill	Input physical quantity	Numbers employed	Hours worked	
	NE				US AU* IC SP NZ	AL	IR
	US NE				UK* AU* SP NZ		IR
			SW		AU* SP NZ	AL	IR TU

MEASUREMENT METHODS OF VALUE ADDED AT CONSTANT PRICES IN SERVICE ACTIVITIES

ISIC Revision 3	Double Indicators			Single indicators		
				Output related indices		
	Double deflation	Double extrapolation	Extrapolation /deflation	Deflated value added	Extrapolated value added	
					Volume	Physical quantity
7411 Legal activities	US JA GE FR CA DE FI NE			BE	LU	UK
7412 Accounting, book-keeping, auditing and tax consultancy	JA GE FR CA DE FI				UK LU	
7413 Market research and public opinion polling	JA GE FR CA FI				LU	
7414 Business and management consultancy	JA GE FR CA FI			IC	LU	

* Identifies indicators adjusted for labour productivity change.

MEASUREMENT METHODS OF VALUE ADDED AT CONSTANT PRICES IN SERVICE ACTIVITIES

Single indicators							Other Methods
Input related indices							
Deflated value added		Extrapolated value added					
Intermediate consumption price	Wage rate	Intermediate consumption volume	Deflated wage bill	Input physical quantity	Numbers employed	Hours worked	
					UK* IC IR		
	US NE				IC IR		
	NE				UK* IC IR		
	US NE				UK* IC IR		

MEASUREMENT METHODS OF VALUE ADDED AT CONSTANT PRICES IN SERVICE ACTIVITIES

ISIC Revision 3		Double Indicators			Single indicators		
						Output related indices	
		Double deflation	Double extrapolation	Extrapolation /deflation	Deflated value added	Extrapolated value added	
						Volume	Physical quantity
742	Architectural, engineering and other technical activities	JA GE FR CA DE FI			BE IC	LU	
743	Advertising	JA GE FR CA DE FI SP			IC	LU	
749	Business activities n.e.c.	JA GE FR CA DE FI			IC	LU	
801-802	Primary and secondary education	US GE FR IT CA DE NO SE			BE		SP

* Identifies indicators adjusted for labour productivity change.

MEASUREMENT METHODS OF VALUE ADDED AT CONSTANT PRICES IN SERVICE ACTIVITIES

Single indicators							Other Methods
Input related indices							
Deflated value added		Extrapolated value added					
Intermediate consumption price	Wage rate	Intermediate consumption volume	Deflated wage bill	Input physical quantity	Numbers employed	Hours worked	
	US NE				UK* IC IR		
	NE				UK* IC IR		
	NE				UK* IC		
		AL			UK* LU	AL	IR NZ

MEASUREMENT METHODS OF VALUE ADDED AT CONSTANT PRICES IN SERVICE ACTIVITIES

ISIC Revision 3	Double Indicators			Single indicators		
				Output related indices		
	Double deflation	Double extrapolation	Extrapolation /deflation	Deflated value added	Extrapolated value added	
					Volume	Physical quantity
803 Higher education	US GE FR IT CA DE NO SE			BE		SP
809 Adult and other education	US JA GE FR IT CA DE NE NO SE		FI (5) SE (6)	AU BE SP		
851 Human health activities	US JA GE FR IT CA BE (1) DE FI NE (2) NO (3) SE (4) SP		NO (7) SE (8)	AU BE (9) IC	BE (10) LU NZ	NZ

* Identifies indicators adjusted for labour productivity change.

NOTES

1. BE   Medical and dental practice.
2. NE   Extra-mural services including non-market services.
3. NO   Hospitals.
4. SE   Dental treatment.
5. FI   Driving schools.
6. SE   Driving schools.

MEASUREMENT METHODS OF VALUE ADDED AT CONSTANT PRICES IN SERVICE ACTIVITIES

Single indicators							Other Methods
Input related indices							
Deflated value added		Extrapolated value added					
Intermediate consumption price	Wage rate	Intermediate consumption volume	Deflated wage bill	Input physical quantity	Numbers employed	Hours worked	
		AL			UK* LU	AL	IR NZ
	NE	AL			UK* LU	AL	IR NZ
NE (11)	NE (11)	AL	AL SW		UK* IC IR NZ	AL	

7. NO Doctors and dental services.
8. SE Private medical treatment.
9. BE Hospital activities.
10. BE Other human health activities.
11. NE Intra-mural services including non-market services.

MEASUREMENT METHODS OF VALUE ADDED AT CONSTANT PRICES IN SERVICE ACTIVITIES

ISIC Revision 3	Double Indicators			Single indicators		
				Output related indices		
	Double deflation	Double extrapolation	Extrapolation /deflation	Deflated value added	Extrapolated value added	
					Volume	Physical quantity
852 Veterinary activities	JA GE FR IT DE NE NO SP			BE	FI LU NZ	
90 Sewage and refuse disposal, sanitation and similar activities	US JA GE FR DE FI NO SE			AU LU		AL
9211 Motion picture and video production and distribution	JA GE FR IT CA DE SE SP	NO		BE LU	UK FI AL	

* Identifies indicators adjusted for labour productivity change.

MEASUREMENT METHODS OF VALUE ADDED AT CONSTANT PRICES IN SERVICE ACTIVITIES

Single indicators							Other Methods
Input related indices							
Deflated value added		Extrapolated value added					
Intermediate consumption price	Wage rate	Intermediate consumption volume	Deflated wage bill	Input physical quantity	Numbers employed	Hours worked	
			SW		UK* AU* IC IR NZ		SE
	NE				UK* SP		
	US				AU NE		

47

MEASUREMENT METHODS OF VALUE ADDED AT CONSTANT PRICES IN SERVICE ACTIVITIES

ISIC Revision 3		Double Indicators			Single indicators		
						Output related indices	
		Double deflation	Double extrapolation	Extrapolation /deflation	Deflated value added	Extrapolated value added	
						Volume	Physical quantity
9212	Motion picture projection	JA GE FR IT CA DE NE SE SP	NO		US (1) BE IC LU	UK AU IR AL	FI
9213	Radio and television activities	US JA GE FR IT CA DE FI NE NO SP		SE	AU BE IC LU	UK AL	IR NZ
9214	Dramatic arts, music and other arts activities	US JA GE FR IT CA DE SE SP	NO		AU BE IC LU	UK IR (2) AL	UK

NOTES

1. US Theatres.
2. IR Theatres.
3. IR Dramatic arts, music and other arts activities other than theatres.

MEASUREMENT METHODS OF VALUE ADDED AT CONSTANT PRICES IN SERVICE ACTIVITIES

Single indicators							Other Methods
Input related indices							
Deflated value added		Extrapolated value added					
Intermediate consumption price	Wage rate	Intermediate consumption volume	Deflated wage bill	Input physical quantity	Numbers employed	Hours worked	
	US				NE		
					IC		
					IC IR (3) NE		

MEASUREMENT METHODS OF VALUE ADDED AT CONSTANT PRICES IN SERVICE ACTIVITIES

ISIC Revision 3		Double Indicators			Single indicators		
						Output related indices	
		Double deflation	Double extrapolation	Extrapolation /deflation	Deflated value added	Extrapolated value added	
						Volume	Physical quantity
9219	Other entertainment activities n.e.c.	US JA GE FR IT CA SE SP			AU BE IC LU	UK IR AL (1)	FI NZ (2)
922	News agency activities	JA GE FR IT SE SP			BE LU	AL	
923	Library, archives, museums and other cultural activities	JA GE FR IT CA DE SE SP	NO		BE LU		

* Identifies indicators adjusted for labour productivity change.

NOTES

1. AL Gambling.
2. NZ Horse and greyhound racing and lotteries.
3. IR Residual parts of other entertainment activities not individually identified to which volume indices of identified elements are applied.

MEASUREMENT METHODS OF VALUE ADDED AT CONSTANT PRICES IN SERVICE ACTIVITIES

Single indicators							Other Methods
Input related indices							
Deflated value added		Extrapolated value added					
Intermediate consumption price	Wage rate	Intermediate consumption volume	Deflated wage bill	Input physical quantity	Numbers employed	Hours worked	
					IC NE		IR (3)
	NE				US AU*		IR
	US				NE		IR

MEASUREMENT METHODS OF VALUE ADDED AT CONSTANT PRICES IN SERVICE ACTIVITIES

ISIC Revision 3	Double Indicators			Single indicators		
				Output related indices		
	Double deflation	Double extrapolation	Extrapolation /deflation	Deflated value added	Extrapolated value added	
					Volume	Physical quantity
924 Sporting and other recreational activities	US JA GE FR IT CA DE NE SE SP		NO	AU BE IC LU	UK FI IR AL	
93 Other service activities	US JA GE FR CA DE NE SP SE			AU BE IC LU SE	UK FI IR AL (2) NZ (3)	SE (4) AL (5)
B. NON MARKET SERVICES						
L. **Public Administration and Defence, compulsory social security**	JA DE NO		IT	NZ (1)	SW	NZ (6)

* Identifies indicators adjusted for labour productivity change.

NOTES

1. NZ Non-government non profit institutions called QUANGOS.
2. AL Hairdressing.
3. NZ Repairs and personal services including motor vehicle repairs.
4. SE Funeral services.
5. AL Funeral services and dry-cleaning services.
6. NZ Accident Compensation Commission.

MEASUREMENT METHODS OF VALUE ADDED AT CONSTANT PRICES IN SERVICE ACTIVITIES

Single indicators							Other Methods
Input related indices							
Deflated value added		Extrapolated value added					
Intermediate consumption price	Wage rate	Intermediate consumption volume	Deflated wage bill	Input physical quantity	Numbers employed	Hours worked	
					NE IC		IR (12)
					UK* IC	AL (2)	NZ (3)
	GE* FR AU (7) BE FI IR NE* PO		UK IC SP NZ (8)		US UK CA AU (9) LU* SP NZ (10)	SE AL (11)	UK CA SP

7. AU Services to the community as a whole except defence and public order and safety.
8. NZ Local government services.
9. AU Defence and public order and safety
10. NZ Other services in category L.
11. AL Excluding services to the community as a whole.
12. IR Concerns elements not individually identified.

MEASUREMENT METHODS OF VALUE ADDED AT CONSTANT PRICES IN SERVICE ACTIVITIES

ISIC Revision 3	Double Indicators			Single indicators		
					Output related indices	
	Double deflation	Double extrapolation	Extrapolation /deflation	Deflated value added	Extrapolated value added	
					Volume	Physical quantity
M. Education	JA DE NO		IT		CA (1) AU (2)	FR IR
73 Research and development	JA NO					
851 Human health activities	JA DE NO		IT			FR UK NZ
853 Social work activities	JA DE	NO				

* Identifies indicators adjusted for labour productivity change.

NOTES

1. CA Universities.
2. AU Adult and other education.
3. US Non government/non-profit operated services.
4. GE Government operated services.
5. CA Other health services.

MEASUREMENT METHODS OF VALUE ADDED AT CONSTANT PRICES IN SERVICE ACTIVITIES

Single indicators							Other Methods
Input related indices							
Deflated value added		Extrapolated value added					
Intermediate consumption price	Wage rate	Intermediate consumption volume	Deflated wage bill	Input physical quantity	Numbers employed	Hours worked	
	GE* BE NE*		PO SP		US GE (6) UK CA (7) AU IR SP	SE	UK CA SP NZ
	US (3) GE* (4) FR NE*				US (8) GE (6) AU	SE	
	US (3) GE* (4) CA (5) NE		UK PO SP	SP	US (8) GE (6) UK CA (9) AU IR	SE	UK CA SP
	US GE* (4) FR CA AU BE		SP		GE (6) UK NE SP	SE	UK CA IR SP

6. GE Private non-profit institutions serving households.
7. CA Primary education only.
8. US Government operated services.
9. CA Hospitals.

MEASUREMENT METHODS OF VALUE ADDED AT CONSTANT PRICES IN SERVICE ACTIVITIES

ISIC Revision 3	Double Indicators			Single indicators		
				Output related indices		
	Double deflation	Double extrapolation	Extrapolation /deflation	Deflated value added	Extrapolated value added	
					Volume	Physical quantity
90 Sewage and refuse disposal, sanitation and similar activities	JA DE					
911 Activities of business, employers and professional organisations	JA DE	NO		BE		
912 Activities of trade unions	JA DE	NO		BE		AU
919 Activities of other membership organisations	JA DE	NO		BE		AU

* Identifies indicators adjusted for labour productivity change.

MEASUREMENT METHODS OF VALUE ADDED AT CONSTANT PRICES IN SERVICE ACTIVITIES

Single indicators							Other Methods
Input related indices							
Deflated value added		Extrapolated value added					
Intermediate consumption price	Wage rate	Intermediate consumption volume	Deflated wage bill	Input physical quantity	Numbers employed	Hours worked	
NE	GE* FR AU BE NE		SP		UK SP	SE	UK SP
	US FR CA AU NE SE				GE IT IR SP		CA NZ
	US FR CA NE SE				GE IT IR SP		CA
	US FR CA NE SE				GE IT IR SP		CA

57

MEASUREMENT METHODS OF VALUE ADDED AT CONSTANT PRICES IN SERVICE ACTIVITIES

ISIC Revision 3	Double Indicators			Single indicators		
					Output related indices	
	Double deflation	Double extrapolation	Extrapolation /deflation	Deflated value added	Extrapolated value added	
					Volume	Physical quantity
92 Recreational, cultural and sporting activities	JA DE	NO				
921 Motion picture, radio, television and other entertainment activities						
923 Library, archives, museums and other cultural activities						
924 Sporting and other recreational activities						
95 Private households with employed persons	JA IT DE			US CA NE NO	IR	

* Identifies indicators adjusted for labour productivity change.

NOTES

1. GE Government operated services.
2. GE Services provided by private non-profit institutions serving households.

MEASUREMENT METHODS OF VALUE ADDED AT CONSTANT PRICES IN SERVICE ACTIVITIES

Single Indicators							Other Methods
Input related indices							
Deflated value added		Extrapolated value added					
Intermediate consumption price	Wage rate	Intermediate consumption volume	Deflated wage bill	Input physical quantity	Numbers employed	Hours worked	
	GE* (1) FR AU				GE (2) UK PO SP	SE UK	
	FR BE				CA NE		CA
	US FR BE				NE		
	FR CA BE				US NE	.	CA
	FR		SW		GE AU BE FI LU SP SE		NZ

ANNEX 3.1
Relative Importance of Different Methods: Shares in Service Value Added

Annex Table 3.1 refers to various years from 1990 to 1993 and shows how much of value added in services is obtained by double and single indicator methods. Column 1 refers to the deflation of both gross output and intermediate inputs; column 2 covers all other double indicator methods, notably when gross output is obtained by extrapolation of base year values. Column 3 covers all single indicator methods that involve deflation of current price value added whatever type of deflator is used; column 4 refers to all methods involving extrapolation of base year value added whatever kind of extrapolator is used.

The bottom row gives the unweighted average shares. These suggest that direct extrapolation of base year value added (column 4) is the most important approach accounting for nearly 40 % of service value added for these 20 countries. Double deflation is the next most important (30% of service value added), and deflation of value added comes third with 23%. Other double indicator methods account only for 8% of value added. In terms of popularity, direct extrapolation is used by 17 countries. Direct deflation is second with 14 countries, followed closely by double deflation which is used by 13. Nine countries use other double indicator methods.

The key finding from this table is the extensive use of single indicator methods. These account for an (unweighted) share of over 60% of total service value added compared to under 40% for double indicator methods. The popularity of single indicator methods, despite the acknowledged theoretical advantages of double indicator methods, may be partly explained by the difficulty of making reliable estimates of intermediate consumption at constant prices. Another reason, however, is that extrapolation of base year value added using employment or hours worked is a popular technique for service activities where output is difficult to define - e.g. public administration and defence - or where output is difficult to measure - e.g. financial and insurance services.

ANNEX TABLE 3.1

SHARE OF CONSTANT PRICE ANNUAL VALUE ADDED IN SERVICE ACTIVITIES
BY ESTIMATION METHOD

	Double Indicator Methods		Single Indicator Methods		
	Double deflation	Other	Direct deflation of value added	Direct extrapolation of value added	TOTAL
	1	2	3	4	
United States	49.6	4.4	20.5	25.5	100.0
Japan	100.0				100.0
Germany	61.5		18.3	20.2	100.0
France	42.5	31.8	25.7		100.0
United Kingdom			7.7	92.3	100.0
Italy	80.4	18.2		1.4	100.0
Canada	72.4		8.1	19.6	100.0
Austria	17.2	38.6		44.2	100.0
Belgium	4.2	0.2	52.1	43.5	100.0
Denmark	100.0				100.0
Finland	28.6	14.5	54.7	2.2	100.0
Iceland			81.4	18.6	100.0
Ireland			10.0	90.0	100.0
Netherlands	26.6	24.5		48.9	100.0
Spain	5.0	0.6	34.3	60.1	100.0
Sweden	20.8	24.8	1.9	52.5	100.0
Switzerland			37.8	62.2	100.0
Turkey			93.6	6.4	100.0
Australia				100.0	100.0
New Zealand			4.5	95.5	100.0
Average shares (unweighted)	30.4	7.9	22.5	39.2	100.0

CHAPTER 4 - **DESCRIPTION OF THE INDICES USED**

This chapter shows, in tabular form, the kinds of deflation and extrapolation indices used by each country for each service activity. For double indicator methods, only one index is described in the table - namely that used to obtain gross output at constant prices.

Six kinds of methods are distinguished in the table:

-   Double deflation: both gross output and intermediate consumption are converted to constant prices by deflating values at current prices.

-   Extrapolation / deflation: these are double indicator methods where either gross output or intermediate consumption are obtained by extrapolating base year values and the other is obtained by deflation.

-   Double extrapolation: both gross output and intermediate consumption are obtained by extrapolating base year values by a volume or physical quantity index.

-   Deflation of value added: these are single indicator methods using various kinds of price deflators.

-   Extrapolation of value added: these are single indicator methods in which base year value added is extrapolated using any kind of physical quantity or volume index.

-   Other methods.

The table is divided into two parts: Part A for market services and Part B for non-market services. The table uses the same two-letter codes for countries as used in Chapter 3.

Annex 4.1 lists the categories and groups of the ISIC Rev.3.

Note: the indices described for **double indicator methods** refers only to those used to derive constant price **gross output.**

PART A: **MARKET SERVICES**

ISIC CODE	ITEM HEADING	DESCRIPTION OF INDEX	COUNTRY

G. Wholesale and retail trade, repair of motor vehicles, motorcycles and personal and household goods

1. DOUGLE DEFLATION

1. DOUBLE DEFLATION

ISIC CODE	ITEM HEADING	DESCRIPTION OF INDEX	COUNTRY
50.	Sale, maintenance and repair of motor vehicles and motor-cycles	Producer price index or implicit price index used to deflate sales by kind of business	US
		Consumer price index (relevant components)	JA, FR, NE, NO
		Weighted average of consumer price index and wholesale price index	IT
		Consumer price index and wholesale price index (relevant components)	FI
part 50 part 5239	Sale, maintenance and repair of motor vehicles and motor-cycles; other retail sale in specialised stores	Implicit price index: average of base and current ratios of wholesale margins in current dollars to producers' value applied to constant price producers' value of commodity flows entering wholesale trade to derive trade margins in constant prices or Average of base and current ratio of retail margins to producer's value applied to constant price producers' value of commodity flows entering retail trade to derive trade margins in constant prices	CA
502	Repair of motor vehicles	Net price index for automobile repairs (wages, spare parts, standard tyres)	DE

51. 52.	Wholesale trade (except motor vehicles and motorcycles); retail trade (except motor vehicles and motorcycles) including repair of personal and household goods	Implicit output price index (obtained by dividing current price gross output index by an output quantity index based on the trade margin)	IT
51.	Wholesale trade (except motor vehicles and motorcycles)	Producer price index or implicit price index	US
		Unit value index	
			JA
		Implicit price index (average of base and current year ratios of wholesale margins in current dollars applied to constant price producers' value of commodity flows entering wholesale trade to derive trade margins in constant prices)	CA
		Wholesale price index or implicit price index (base year wholesale trade margin ratio applied to constant price commodity flows entering wholesale trade to obtain trade margins in constant prices)	DE
		Wholesale price index (relevant components)	FI
		Implicit price index (base year wholesale trade margin ratio applied to constant price commodity flows entering wholesale trade to obtain trade margins in constant prices)	NE, NO
52.	Retail trade (except motor vehicles and motorcycles, including repair of personal and household goods)	Consumer price index	US
		Consumer price index (relevant components)	FI
		Unit value index	
			JA
M		Implicit price index (base year retail margin ratio applied to constant price flows of goods entering retail trade to derive trade margins in constant prices)	DE, NE, NO
52. (exc. part 5239 part 5260	Retail trade, except for motor vehicles and motorcycles, part of repair of personal and household goods and part of other retail sales in specialised stores	Implicit price index (average base and current year retail margins on current values applied to constant price producers' value of commodity flows entering retail trade to derive trade margins in constant prices)	CA

part 5260	Part of repair of personal and household goods	Composite index of relevant consumer price indices and indices of average weekly earnings	CA

2. EXTRAPOLATION/DEFLATION

51. 52.	Wholesale trade (except motor vehicles and motorcycles) and retail trade (except motor vehicles and motorcycles; repair of personal and household goods)	Volume index of products sold	FR
		Output volume index obtained from deflated sales in different types of stores	NZ

3. DEFLATION OF VALUE ADDED

50.	Sale, maintenance and repair of motor vehicles and motorcycles	Combination of specific producer price and consumer price indices	UK
part 50	Sale, maintenance and repair of motor vehicles and motorcycles (except repair services)	Consumer price index (relevant components)	AU, IC
51.	Wholesale trade (except motor vehicles and motorcycles)	Wholesale price index	AU
		Average retail trade price index	IC
52.	Retail trade (except motor vehicles and motorcycles, and repair services)	Consumer price index (relevant components)	IC
part 52	Retail trade (except motor vehicles and motorcycles) excluding repair services	Consumer price index (relevant components)	AU

4. EXTRAPOLATION OF VALUE ADDED

G.	Wholesale and retail trade (including repair of motor vehicles, motorcycles and personal and household goods)	Output volume index obtained by deflation using selling price indices of wholesale and retail trade	GE
		Weighted average of volume indices of components of personal expenditure and gross fixed capital formation	IR
		Consumption volume index of traded goods	SP

		Output volume index to which the ratio of value added to output is applied	TU
50.	Sale, maintenance and repair of motor vehicles and motorcycles	Physical quantity index based on new motor vehicle registrations	AL
5050.	Retail sale of automotive fuel	Physical quantity index based on deliveries of petroleum products	BE
51. 52. (exc. 526)	Wholesale trade and commission trade, except of motor vehicles and motorcycles; retail trade except of motor vehicles and motorcycles	Implicit volume index of private consumption expenditure on traded goods	BE
51.	Wholesale trade (except motor vehicles and motorcycles)	Physical quantity output index of agricultural and energy products for household goods and constant price turnover index obtained by deflation using producer price indices for other industrial materials, food and drink and consumer goods	UK
		Composite index of deflated sales by appropriate consumer price index components and index of numbers employed	PO
		Index of constant price sales of wholesale enterprises	SW, AL
52.	Retail trade except of motor vehicles and motorcycles; repair of personal and household goods	Constant price turnover index obtained by deflation using appropriate components of the retail price index	UK
		Composite index of deflated sales by appropriate components of the consumer price index and index of numbers employed	PO
		Deflated retail sales index by consumer price index	SW
		Index of constant price turnover of retail establishments	AL

5. OTHER METHOD

A. CONTROLLED DOUBLE DEFLATION or EXTRAPOLATION/DEFLATION

(A preliminary estimate of constant price value added is obtained as a residual between constant price gross output and calculated intermediate consumption assuming fixed input coefficients in constant prices. Intermediate consumption is then adjusted in an input/output system so that supply equals demand for all service commodity groups. Constant price gross output is obtained either by deflation or extrapolation, as described in column 3)

part 50 51. part 52	Sale and maintenance of motor vehicles and motorcycles (except repairs); retail sale of automotive fuel; wholesale trade and commission trade, except of motor vehicles and motorcycles; retail trade, except of motor vehicles and motorcycles (except repairs of personal and household goods)	Constant price trade margins obtained from I-O calculations as fixed part of final and intermediate demand	SE
502.	Maintenance and repair of motor vehicles	Index of number of cars, buses and lorries used to extrapolate gross output	SE
526.	Repair of personal and household goods	Consumer price index of repair of personal and household goods used to deflate gross output	SE

B. PART DOUBLE EXTRAPOLATION, PART EXTRAPOLATION/DEFLATION

50. (exc. 5050)	Sale, maintenance and repair of motor vehicles and motorcycles	Specific price indices (used to deflate trade margins), relevant components of the consumer price index (used to deflate maintenance and repair services), physical quantity index based on number of cars put in circulation (used to extrapolate sales of second-hand cars)	BE

H. Hotels and restaurants

1. DOUBLE DEFLATION

55.	Hotels and restaurants	Consumer price index (relevant components)	GE, FR, IT, FI, NE
		Net price index (consumer price index corrected for indirect taxation)	DE
551.	Hotels, camping sites and other short stay accommodation	Room rate index	US
		Consumer price index and corporate service price index (for hotel rates)	JA
		Consumer price index (relevant components)	CA, NO
552.	Restaurants, bars and canteens	Consumer price index (relevant components)	US, JA
		Consumer price index (tax adjusted relevant components)	CA
part 552	Restaurants, bars and canteens (food)	Consumer price index (relevant components relating to restaurants)	NO

2. EXTRAPOLATION/DEFLATION

part 552	Restaurants, bars and canteens (drinks)	Physical quantity index of drinks consumed	NO

3. DEFLATION OF VALUE ADDED

55.	Hotels and restaurants	Retail price index (relevant components)	UK
		Implicit price index of private consumption	BE
		Consumer price index (relevant components)	TU
551.	Hotels, camping sites and other short stay accommodation	Weighted average of general consumer price index and relevant items of consumer price index	IC
part 551	Hotels, camping sites and other short stay accommodation	Consumer price index (relevant components)	AU
552.	Restaurants, bars and canteens	Consumer price index (relevant components)	AU, IC

4. EXTRAPOLATION OF VALUE ADDED

55.	Hotels and restaurants	Index of deflated sales (consumer price index relevant components used as deflator)	LU
		Physical quantity output index based on number of nights spent in hotels	SW
		Index of deflated sales	NZ
551.	Hotels, camping sites and other short stay accommodation	Physical quantity weighted index of out-of-state visitors and numbers of home holidays	IR
		Physical quantity output index	SP, AL
part 551	Private lodging	Physical quantity output index based on number of nights spent	AU
552.	Restaurants, bars and canteens	Index of numbers employed	IR, SP
		Constant price turnover index and constant price private final consumption expenditure index	AL

5. OTHER METHOD

CONTROLLED DOUBLE DEFLATION

| 55. | Hotels and restaurants | Consumer price index (relevant components) | SE |

I.   Transport, storage and communications

Transport and storage

1. DOUBLE DEFLATION

A. Passenger transport

60. 612. 62.	Land, inland water and air transport	Implicit output price index (output volume index derived from index of passenger kilometres)	GE
601. 62.	Rail and air transport	Implicit output price index (output volume index based on passenger-kilometres)	NE
612.	Inland water transport	Implicit output price index (output volume index based on number of passengers transported)	NE
611.	Sea transport	Implicit output price index (output volume index based on various types of volume indices)	NE
601. 602. 61.	Rail, other land, water transport	Net price indices (for rail fares, buses, coaches, tramways, taxis and ferries), tariffs (for sight-seeing buses)	DE
		Composite output price index of implicit price index (output volume index of passenger-kilometres) and consumer price index	NE
62.	Air transport	Price index for charter and regular flights for personal and business travel	CA
		Weighted price index of: net price index (for domestic flights), output price index (output volume index based on passenger-kilometres) and expenditure index (for charter flights)	DE
601. 611. 62.	Rail, sea and air transport	Consumer price index (for rail, sea and air transport of passengers)	IT
601 602 61	Rail, other land and water transport	Consumer price index (for rail passenger travel, urban transit, international and rural transit, taxicabs, other transit, ferry services)	CA

71

601. 602. part 62	Rail, other land and domestic air transport	Consumer price index (relevant components)	JA
601. 612. 62.	Rail, inland water and air transport	Consumer price index (components for rail, boat and ferry and air transport respectively)	NO
62.	Air transport	Consumer price index for passenger air transport	SE
612. part 62	Inland water and international air transport	Corporate service price index	JA
611.	Sea transport	Unit value index	JA
		Estimated price indices based on volume (tonnage) and income (gross rates)	NO
601.	Rail transport	Output price index	SE
		Official tariff index	SP

B. Freight transport

60. 612. 62.	Land, pipeline, inland water and air freight transport	Implicit output price index (output volume index derived from index of tonne-kilometres carried)	GE
601. 611. 62.	Rail, sea and air transport	Implicit output price index obtained by dividing the current price output index by a quantity index based on tonne-kilometres carried	IT
601. 61. 62.	Rail, water and air freight transport	Implicit output price index (output volume index based on number of tonnes transported)	DE
601.	Rail freight transport	Unit value index	JA
		Implicit price index based on unit value indices of interprovincial and Canada/US freight revenue per tonne-kilometres	CA
		Official tariff index	SP
611. 612.	Sea, inland water transport	Implicit output price index (output volume index based on shipping tonnage)	CA
611.	Sea freight transport	Unit value index and corporate service price index	JA
		Implicit output price index (output volume based on various types of volume indices)	NE

		Estimated price indices based on volume (tonnage) and income (gross rates) by type and size of vessel	NO
		Price indices of international freight	SE
602. 612. 62.	Other land, inland water and air freight transport	Corporate service price index	JA
602.	Other land freight transport	Tariff indices for truck transport	DE
612.	Inland water freight transport	Combined price index of consumer price index, price index for land transport and wage rate index	NO
62.	Air transport	Implicit price index based on unit value indices of freight revenue per tonne-kilometre by distance block (or volume index based on tonnes transported)	CA

C. Passenger and freight transport

602. 603. 612.	Other land, inland water freight and pipeline transport	Weighted average of: price index for "transport and freight" and implicit output price index (output volume index based on number of vehicle-kilometres on motorways)	IT
611.	Sea transport	Sea freight cost index	GE, BE
62.	Air transport	Consumer price index for air transport	NO

D. Supporting and auxiliary transport activities, activities of travel agencies

63.	Supporting and auxiliary transport activities, activities of travel agencies	Consumer price index (rail and air fares and hotel rates)	JA
		Special estimated price index obtained from price indices of intermediate consumption goods and wage indices of these industries	GE
		Producer price index	FR
		Consumer price index for motorway tolls and parkings	IT
		Implicit price index (output volume index based on various types of volume indices)	NE
part 63.	Relating to land transport	Net consumer price index	DE

	Relating to water transport	Price index based on wharfage handling cost, pilotage, harbour dues and services incidental to water transport	CA
		Implicit price index and weighted price index	DE
	Relating to air transport	Index of average weekly earnings	CA
	Relating to warehousing	Price index based on volume of elevator activity by type of grain weighted by base year prices and index of average weekly earnings	CA
		Average of wage rate index and net consumer price index (for electricity)	DE
	Relating to travel agencies and parkings	Consumer price index (relevant components)	CA

2. DOUBLE EXTRAPOLATION

A. Passenger and freight transport

62.	Air transport	Physical quantity output index of tonne-kilometres transported	BE

B. Freight transport

602.	Other land transport	Average output volume index of tonne-kilometres carried, sales of diesel oil and turnover of hired truck transport deflated by a cost price index	NO
601. 603.	Rail and pipeline transport	Physical quantity index of tonne-kilometres carried	NO

3. EXTRAPOLATION/DEFLATION

A. Passenger transport

601. 602. 61. 62.	Land, water and air transport	Physical quantity output index	FR
602.	Other land transport	Physical quantity output index of passenger-miles (for intercity bus transport), of employment (for school buses), number of passenger trips (for other land transport) and private consumption expenditure deflated by consumer price index for taxi fares	US

74

		Composite index of number of licences issued, kilometres operated and deflated turnover by consumer price index (for taxicabs) and deflated turnover by consumer price index (for buses)	NO
		Composite physical quantity output index based on number of passengers, passenger-kilometres and number of vehicles	SP
611.	Sea transport	Physical quantity output index based on number of passengers from abroad	SE

B. Freight transport

60. 61. 62.	Land (including pipeline) water and air transport	Physical quantity output index	FR
602. 603.	Other land, transport via pipelines	Physical quantity index of tonne-miles	US
part 602	Other land transport	Volume index based on tonnes transported (or implicit price index based on unit value indices of freight revenue per tonne-kilometres by distance block)	CA
603.	Transport via pipelines	Volume index of products carried	CA
601. 62.	Rail and air transport	Physical quantity output index of tonne-kilometres	SE

C. Passenger and freight

601.	Rail transport	Physical quantity output index of passenger-miles and tonne-miles	US
62.	Air transport	Physical quantity output index of passenger-miles and tonne miles	US

D. Supporting and auxiliary transport activities, activities of travel agencies

63.	Supporting and auxiliary transport activities, activities of travel agencies	Volume index of imports and exports combined (exc. ships) for expedition and output volume index for manufacturing. Output index deflated by consumer price index (average dwellings, repairs) and wage price index for transport centrals, composite volume index based on number of automobiles and deflated output by consumer price index and wage rate index for other services	NO

4. DEFLATION OF VALUE ADDED

A. Passenger transport

602. 611.	Other land and see transport	Consumer price index (relevant components)	TU
602.	Other land transport	Consumption price index (relevant components)	AU, IC
part 602	Other land transport	Tariff indices (for buses)	FI
61.	Water transport	Consumer price index (relevant components)	FI

B. Freight transport

602.	Other land transport	Consumer price index (relevant components)	AU
603.	Transport via pipelines	Consumer price index (relevant components)	TU
		Implicit output price index (calculated from current gross output and volume of cargo carried)	NZ

C. Passenger and freight

601. 62.	Transport via railways, air transport	Consumer price index (relevant components)	TU
602.	Other land transport	Implicit output price index (calculated from current and constant price revenue of road passenger and freight transport and allied services by sector. Deflators used are producer price indices)	NZ
62.	Air transport	Implicit output price index (current output values deflated by various price indices)	IC
part 62	Air transport	Implicit output price deflator (for 2nd and 3rd level air transport operators)	NZ

D. Supporting and auxiliary transport activities, activities of travel agencies

63.	Supporting and auxiliary transport activities, activities of travel agencies	Freight tariff index	AU
		Consumer price index (relevant components for railway station services and travel agencies)	FI

		Tariff indices (for stevedoring, forwarding and ports)	FI
		Consumer price index (relevant components)	SP
part 63	Supporting and auxiliary transport activities, activities of travel agencies	Implicit output price index (gross output deflated by producer price indices of airport operation) for supporting air transport operation	NZ

5. EXTRAPOLATION OF VALUE ADDED

A. Passenger transport

601.	Rail transport	Physical quantity output index of passenger-kilometres	UK, AU, FI, IR, LU, PO
		Output volume index (constant price final consumption expenditure on rail fares)	AL
		Output volume index (constant price output deflated by price index of urban and interurban rail passenger fares)	NZ
602.	Other land transport	Output volume index (turnover of taxi operators deflated by specific consumer price index)	UK
		Physical quantity output index of passenger journeys and vehicle kilometres (for state owned bus transport), of seating capacity (for private bus transport); input physical quantity index based on number of taxis; index of number of state visitors (for car hire)	IR
		Output volume index (current price output deflated by consumer price index for public transport)	LU
		Physical quantity output index of passenger-kilometres	PO
		Constant price final consumption expenditure index (for buses, trams and taxis)	AL
part 602	Other land transport (taxis)	Output physical quantity index based on number of taxis and number of employed	FI
611.	Sea transport	Output volume index (international passenger revenue deflated by specific consumer price index)	UK
		Average volume index of volume index of output (deflated by GDP price index), volume index of exports and volume index of imports	IC

		Physical quantity output index of travellers by sea	IR
		Physical quantity output index of number of passengers transported	PO
612.	Inland water trandpoirt	Physical quantity output index of number of passengers transported	AU, LU
62.	Air transport	Physical quantity output index based on passenger-kilometres	AU, AL
		Physical quantity output index of passenger-kilometres (for state owned air transport); output volume index obtained by deflating receipts by implicit price index for state company (for private owned air transport)	IR
		Physical quantity output index of number of passengers transported	PO

B. Freight transport

601.	Rail transport	Physical quantity index of tonne-kilometres carried	AU, IR, LU, PO, NZ
		Index of tonne-kilometres of freight carried (public) and tonnes of freight carried (private)	AL
602.	Other land transport	Physical quantity output index based on number of lorries and number employed for chartered transport and on tonne-kilometres for scheduled transport	FI
		Physical quantity output index of tonne-kilometres carried	IR
		Output volume index (current price output deflated by consumer price index)	LU
		Physical quantity output index based on tonne-kilometres of freight carried for hire or reward	AL
part 602 part 611	Other land transport of freight; sea transport of freight	Output volume index to which the ratio of value added to output is applied	TU
603.	Transport via pipelines	Output physical quantity index based on tonne-kilometres	AU
611.	Sea transport	Output volume index (receipts deflated by specific output price index)	UK

		Physical quantity weighted average index of tonnes of goods and numbers of live animals carried	IR
		Physical quantity output index of tonnes carried	PO
		Physical quantity output index of revenue tonnes of coastal and overseas cargo carried by Australian registered ships	AL
		Output volume index (deflated by price index of freight rates)	NZ
612.	Inland water transport	Physical quantity output index of tonnage carried	AU, LU
62.	Air transport	Physical quantity output index based on tonne-kilometres	AU, AL
		Output physical quantity index of tonnes-kilometres	IR
		Physical quantity output index of tonnes carried	PO

C. Passenger and freight transport

60. 61. 62. 63. 64.	Transport and storage	Output volume index based on number of passengers and freight volume transported	SW
601.	Rail transport	Physical quantity index of tonne-kilometres carried	UK
		Weighted physical quantity index based on number of passenger-kilometres, tonne-kilometres and deflated own account capital formation	BE
61.	Water transport	Index of number of persons employed	US
611.	Sea transport	Physical quantity index of volume of cargo and number of passengers carried	NZ
part 62	Air transport	Physical quantity output index based on revenue passenger-kilometres and revenue tonne-kilometres split between domestic and international air transport, weighted by base year revenue	NZ

63.	Supporting and auxiliary transport activities, activities of travel agencies	Index of number of persons employed	US
		Output volume index (turnover deflated by consumer price index)	UK
		Implied volume index for rest of the transport sector	IR
		Physical quantity output index of tonnage handled, for river ports, or physical quantity output index of number of persons frequenting airports, for supporting services to air transport, or output volume index (current price output deflated by consumer price index), for other services	LU
part 63	Supporting and auxiliary transport activities, activities of travel agencies	Physical quantity index of volume of cargo handled in harbours	BE
	Supporting and auxiliary sea, air and road transport activities	Output volume index (receipts deflated by specific output price indices)	AL
		Physical quantity output index of volume of shipping through ports and of volume of cargo handled (for harbours); of volume of cargo handled (for stevedoring)	NZ

6. OTHER METHOD:

CONTROLLED DOUBLE DEFLATION or EXTRAPOLATION/DEFLATION

(A preliminary estimate of constant price value added is obtained as a residual between constant price gross output and calculated intermediate consumption assuming fixed input coefficients in constant prices. Intermediate consumption is then adjusted in an input/output system so that supply equals demand for all service commodity groups. Constant price gross output is obtained either by deflation or extrapolation as described in column 3)

A. Passenger transport

part 602	Other land transport (buses)	Consumer price index (for local transport) used to deflate gross output	SE
	(taxis)	Number of taxi cabs used to extrapolate gross output	SE

B. Freight transport

| 602. | Other land transport | Cost index based on intermediate consumption price index and on wage rate index used to deflate gross output | SE |

C. Passenger and freight

| 612. | Inland and water transport | Consumer price index for inland passenger transport used to deflate gross output | SE |

D. Supporting and auxiliary transport activities, activities of travel agencies

| 63. | Supporting and auxiliary transport activities, activities of travel agencies | Constant price output index calculated from output of rail, land freight, sea and air transport used as indicators | SE |

Post and Telecommunications

1. DOUBLE DEFLATION

64.	Post and telecommunica-tions	Consumer price index (relevant components)	JA, IT, NO
		Special price indices of post and telecommunication charges	GE
		Output volume indices, consumer price index, wholesale price index and construction price indices	AU
		Net consumer price indices	DE
		Implicit output price index	NE
641.	Post and courier activities	Consumer price index (relevant components)	SE
642.	Telecommunications	Composite index of producer price indices of local and toll calls and of directory advertising	US
		Price index of telephone rates	SE
part 642	Cable TV	Consumer price index for cable TV	CA

2. EXTRAPOLATION/DEFLATION

| 64. | Post and telecommunica-tions | Output physical quantity index | FR |
| 641. | Post and courier activities | Output volume index (implicit price index used as deflator) | CA |

642.	Communications (exc. cable TV)	Output volume index (implicit price index used as deflator)	CA

3. DEFLATION OF VALUE ADDED

64.	Post and telecommunica-tions	Income volume index (specific price indices used as deflators)	IC
		Consumer price index (relevant components)	TU
641.	Post and courier activities	Price index of postal tariffs	BE
642.	Telecommunications	Consumer price index of phone calls	FI
part 642	Telegraph and telephone	Consumer price index (relevant components)	BE
	Radio and TV	Wage rate index	BE

4. EXTRAPOLATION OF VALUE ADDED

64.	Post and telecommunica-tions	Output physical quantity index	LU
		Index of constant price income of post, telegraph and telephone (consumer price index for communications used as deflator)	SW
641.	Post and courier activities	Output physical quantity index	US
		Physical quantity output index based on volume of mail and other services provided by UK Post Office	UK
		Income volume index of post and courier activities	FI
		Physical quantity output index based on numbers of items delivered (state company); index of numbers employed (private sector)	IR
		Physical quantity output index based on number of items and new services delivered	PO
		Output volume index derived by quantity revaluation (for mail and postal services) or price deflation (for other postal services)	AL
		Physical quantity output index based on number of articles carried	NZ
642.	Communications	Constant price turnover index (specific consumer price index used as deflator)	UK

		Physical quantity weighted average output index based on phone calls, telexes, etc.	IR
		Physical quantity output index based on numbers of telephone calls, telexes and new services	PO
part 642	Telephone rentals and connections	Output physical quantity index derived by quantity revaluation	AL
	Phone calls and other revenue	Output volume index (relevant components of the consumer price index used as deflators)	AL
	International tolls	Output physical quantity index based on number of calls minutes	NZ
	Domestic tolls	Output volume index (relevant price indices used as deflators of revenue)	NZ
	Own account capital formation	Index of hours worked	NZ

5. OTHER METHOD

PART DOUBLE DEFLATION, PART EXTRAPOLATION OF VALUE ADDED

641.	Post and courier activities	Price index of postal rates and output physical quantity index based on postal traffic	SP
642.	Telecommunications	Price index of telephone rates, and output physical quantity index based on number of telephone calls	SP

J. **Financial intermediation**

1. DOUBLE DEFLATION

65. 66. 67.	Financial intermediation	Producer price index	FR
65. 6601. 67.	Financial intermediation except insurance and pension funding; life insurance; activities auxiliary to financial intermediation	Unit value index	JA
65. 6601.	Financial intermediation except insurence and pension funding; life insurance	Weighted average wage rate index and net price index	DE

65.	Financial intermediation except insurance and pension funding	Implicit price index (obtained from deflated total weighted value of assets and liabilities and deflated explicit service charges)	CA
part 65	Financial intermediation except insurance and pension funding (exc. imputed bank services)	Special price index by kind of service	GE
		Domestic demand price deflator	IT
	Imputed bank services	Special price index: current year domestic demand deflator (Dt) is multiplied by the ratio of indices of the interest margin (m) to the value of intermediation by the Bank of Italy (M) for the current and base year period (respectively t and o). Deflator of imputed bank services;	IT

$$DIBS = \frac{Dt.mt \, / \, Mt}{mo \, / \, Mo}$$

part 651	The interest margin	Composite price index (obtained by multiplying the price index of demand by the interest spread)	FI
part 651 659. 67.	Monetary intermediation (exc. the interest margin), other financial intermediation, activities auxiliary to financial intermediation	Weighted average of wage rate index and financial services cost index included in CPI	FI
660. 672.	Insurance and pension funding except compulsory social security; activities auxiliary to insurance and pension funding	Implicit price index for private consomption expenditure (relevant components)	US
660.	Life insurance; other insurance (except compulsory social security)	Implicit output price index obtained by dividing current price index by a quantity index based on number of insurance contracts	IT
part 66	Compulsory private insurance	Wage rate index	FI
6601.	Life insurance	Implicit output price index (output volume is obtained by extrapolation of base year output; volume indices are obtained by deflation using the consumer price index)	GE

6602. 6603. 67.	Pension funding; non life insurance; activities auxiliary to financial intermediation	Weighted average industrial workers'wage rate index, consumer price index (for casualty insurance), net consumer price index (for automobile insurance), construction price index for one-family houses	DE
6602. 6603.	Pension funding, non life insurance	Corporate service price index and consumer price index (for fire and automobile insurance premiums)	JA
		Implicit output price index (output volume is obtained by extrapoling base year output; volume indicators are obtained by deflation using special price indices)	GE
		Implicit output price index (obtained from deflated premium for property and casualty insurance, from number of persons covered weighted by base year premiums for accidental sickness)	CA
6602.	Voluntary insurance	Consumer price index and wholesale price index of the objects insured	FI
part 6603	Motor vehicle insurance	Consumer price index (for car insurance)	NO
67.	Activities auxiliary to financial intermediation	Special estimated price index obtained from price indices of internediate consumption goods and wage indices of the industry.	GE
		Various price indices of rent, consumer price index (relevant components), implicit price index for commissions of brokers and dealers	DE
671.	Activities auxiliary to financial intermediation, except insurance and pension funding	Implicit price index of securities commissions (for mutual fund sales), implicit GNP price index (for other revenues, security exchanges), composite index of implicit price deflators for commissions, underwriting and GNP (for commodity brokers, dealers, and exchanges of securities and commodities)	US

2. EXTRAPOLATION/DEFLATION

part 65	Imputed bank services	Volume index of the sum of credits and debits of financial institutions (price index of national final uses is used as deflator)	GE

| 651. | Monetary intermediation | Volume index of deposits | LU |
| part 67 | Security brokers and dealers | Output physical quantity index (number of public security orders) | US |

3. DEFLATION OF VALUE ADDED

65. 66. 67.	Financial intermediation	Implicit output price index (specific price indices or general consumer price index used to deflate components of output)	BE
		Consumer price index of services excluding rents	SP
65.	Financial intermediation except insurance and pension funding	Consumer price index excluding rents	PO
6601.	Life insurance	Volume index of administrative costs (average earnings index is used as deflator)	UK
6602. 6603. 67.	Pension funding; non-life insurance; activities auxiliary to financial intermediation	Consumer price index (relevant components)	AU

4. EXTRAPOLATION OF VALUE ADDED

65. 66. 67.	Financial intermediation	Average of deflated wage bill index and of index of man-years worked	IC
		Weighted volume index of intermediate consumption and deflated wage bill	NE
		Index of number of hours worked adjusted for 2% increase in productivity	SE
		Index of number of hours worked	AL
65. 66. 67.	Financial intermediation	Index of numbers employed	TU
65.	Financial intermediation except insurance and pension funding	Various output volume indices	AU
651.	Monetary intermediation	Index of numbers employed	US
		Output volume index (retail price index used as deflator of deposits/loans) and output physical quantity index of number of transactions and index of numbers employed adjusted for productivity change	UK

		Output volume index (GDP price index used to deflate earnings)	SW
part 651 659.	Monetary intermediation; other financial intermediation	Output volume index based on deflated funding and claims and number of cheque account, credit card, ATM and EFT-POS transactions	NZ
part 651	Reserve Bank	Index of average numbers employed	NZ
659.	Other financial intermediation	Output volume index (retail price index used as deflator for building society liabilities) and output physical quantity index of number of advances made by building societies and index of numbers employed	UK
		Volume index of deposits in resident establishments (prices and exchange rates are kept constant)	LU
66.	Insurance and pension funding, except compulsory social security	Output physical quantity index (based on number of contracts	LU
		Output volume index obtained by deflating premium income by the consumer price index component for insurance	SW
		Output volume index based on deflated sums assured (life and fine insurance) or deflated premiums (motor, personal and other accident insurance) or deflated commissions paid	NZ
6601.	Life insurance	Output physical quantity index (number of contracts)	AU
6602. 6603.	Pension funding; non-life insurance	Volume index of total premiums net of reinsurance (specific consumer price index used as deflator)	UK
67.	Activities auxiliary to financial intermediation	Output volume index of total premiums net of reinsurance (specific consumer price index used as deflator) and output physical quantity index of number of transactions in securities	UK
		Output volume index (consumer price index used as deflator)	LU
part 67	Holding and other investment companies	Index of number of persons employed	US

5. OTHER METHOD:

PART DEFLATION, PART EXTRAPOLATION OF GROSS OUTPUT

65. part 66	Financial intermediation except insurance and pension funding; insurance and pension funding (except motor vehicle insurance)	Index of man-hours worked; consumer price index of gross rents for commercial buildings	NO
6601.	Life insurance	Output volume index obtained by deflating premium income for each type of insurance by all-items CPI multiplied by base year unit costs for issuing the various types of insurance (used as weights). Results are summed and a volume index obtained on which the base year value of output is projected	CA

K   **Real estate, renting and business activities**

Real estate

1. DOUBLE DEFLATION

70.	Real estate activities	Price index of rents	NE
		Consumer price index for gross rents	NO, SP
part 70	Owner occupied and rented dwellings	Price index of rents	GE
		Consumer price index	FR
		Implicit price index of households' domestic final consumption	IT
		Paasche-type chain price index based on square metre prices of rented dwellings stratified according to a set of criteria	AU
		Weighted average of index of rents for existing dwellings and index of rents for new dwellings	DE
	Owner occupied dwellings	Implicit price index for imputed rents (constructed using a volume index of space and consumer price index for water and factors for the amount of owner occupied housing)	CA
	Rented dwellings and other real estate activities	Corporate service price index (for office, shop and hotel rents)	JA

	Other real estate activities	Special estimated price index obtained from price indices of intermediate consumption goods and wage indices of these industries	GE
		Producer price index	FR
		Implicit price index obtained by dividing current price output of non residential buildings by a constant price output index of buildings calculated from the constant price change in the stock of buildings	IT
		Average commissions price index on sales of one-family houses	DE

2. EXTRAPOLATION/DEFLATION

| part 70 | Owner occupied and rented dwellings | Output volume index of stock of dwellings (taking into account the quality standard of dwellings) | FI |
| | Other real estate activities | Output volume index based on the stock of buildings other than dwellings owned by real estate companies (for renting); output volume index based on the stock of dwellings owned by real estate companies (for managing and caretaking); or the number of deals concluded (for real estate agents) | FI |

3. DEFLATION OF VALUE ADDED

70.	Real estate activities	Price index of rental values	US
part 70	Other real estate activities	Consumer price index (relevant components)	AU
		Consumer price index (for services)	BE
		Consumer price index	IC
	Rented dwellings	Consumer price index for rents of state housing	IR
	Owner occupied and rented dwellings	Consumer price index (relevant components)	TU

4. EXTRAPOLATION OF VALUE ADDED

| 70. | Real estate activities | Output volume index (consumer price index for rents or construction price index used to deflate output) | LU |
| | | Index of deflated wage bill (consumer price index for private services used as deflator) | SW |

part 70	Owner occupied and rented dwellings	Volume index of stock of residential dwellings including allowance for quality changes	UK
		Composite output volume index taking into account the number of households and quality change in construction and transformation of dwellings	BE
		Output volume index of the mean stock of dwellings calculated using the perpetual inventory method applied to capital formation deflated by a house price index	IR
		Output physical volume index (based on perpetual inventory model of stock of dwellings and imputed rent for owner occupiers)	AL
		Output physical quantity index (average number of owner occupied permanent dwellings or average number of rented dwellings)	NZ
	Owner occupied dwellings	Output volume index of net stock of residential buildings	IC
	Commercial buildings	Output volume index (producer price index of commercial property rental used as deflator)	NZ
	Other real estate	Volume index based on relevant stamp duty payments deflated by components of the Building and Construction index	IR
		Output physical quantity index based on stock of buildings other than dwellings owned by real estate agents (for renting, managing and caretaking) or on the number of deals concluded (for real estate agents)	NZ
		Output volume index to which the ratio of value added to output is applied	TU
		Index of hours worked	AL
	House and estate agents	Output physical quantity index (number of property transactions)	UK
	Owning and dealing in real estate	Volume index of gross capital stock of relevant building at 1990 prices and index of non-trading capital consumption of local authorities and index of number of employees in housing departments	UK

5. OTHER METHOD:

CONTROLLED DOUBLE DEFLATION or EXTRAPOLATION/DEFLATION

(A preliminary estimate of constant price value added is obtained as a residual between constant price gross output and calculated intermediate consumption assuming fixed input coefficients in constant prices. Intermediate consumption is then adjusted in an input/output system so that supply equals demand for all service commodity groups. Constant price gross output is obtained eigher by deflation or extrapolation, as described in column 3)

part 70	Owner occupied dwellings	Stock of 1 and 2 family houses used to extrapolate gross output	SE
	Rented dwellings	Stock of rented dwellings used to extrapolate gross output	SE
	Other real estate activities	Stock used to extrapolate gross output	SE

Renting and business services

1. DOUBLE DEFLATION

71. 72. 73. 74.	Renting of machinery and equipment without operator and of personal and households goods; computer and related activities; research and development; other business services	Wage rate index Building cost index for architectural, engineering and other technical activities; weighted input cost index and wage rate index for other activities	NO FI
71. 72. 73. part 74	Renting of machinery and equipment without operator and of personal and household goods; computer and related activities; research and development; other business services	Special estimated price index obtained from price indices of intermediate consumption goods and wage indices of these industries	GE
part 71 72. 73. 74.	Renting of machinery and equipment without operator and of personal and household goods; computer and related activities; research and development; other business services	Producer price indices	FR
71. 72. 74.	Renting of machinery and equipment without operator and of personal and household goods; computer and related activities; other business services	Weighted average consumer price index of legal services, advertising and car insurance	IT

711. 72. part 74	Renting of transport equipment; computer and related activities; other business services	Corporate service price index (for car rentals, information, legal and accounting services)	JA
712. 73. part 74.	Renting of other machinery and equipment; research and development; other business services	Input cost index	JA
711. 7411.	Renting of transport equipment; legal activities	Consumer price index (relevant components)	US, NE
71.	Renting of machinery and equipment without operator and of personal and household goods	Consumer price index (for automobile and truck rental), machinery and equipment price index (for rental of other machinery and equipment), average weekly earnings index (for other services to business and persons)	CA
712.	Renting of other machinery and equipment	Weighted average wholesale price index	DE
713.	Renting of personal and household goods	Consumer price index (for video rentals)	JA
		Consumer price index (relevant components)	FR
72.	Computer and related activities	Implicit price index based on weighted price for mainframe software, micro software, consulting services, data input services, data base services, computer leasing, system maintenance, customs programming and training	CA
		Price index for selected computer runs	DE
part 73 part 74	Research and development; other business activities	Average price index of implicit price index of legal activities, average weekly earnings index of accountants, engineers and architects	CA
part 74	Other business activities	Index of building costs (for architectural, engineering and other technical services)	GE
		Index of average weekly earnings or weighted implicit price index based on average cost at print medium, radio and TV advertising and outdoor advertising or tax adjusted consumer price index for photographers and consumer price index for repair services	CA

| | | Weighted average of price index for advertising in newspapers, magazines, index of printing costs and wage index or weighted average of fee index related to purchase of 1-family houses and wage index of salary earners or weighted average index of construction costs and wage index (for architectural and engineering activities) or wage index of net consumer price index | DE |

2. DEFLATION OF VALUE ADDED

71.	Renting of machinery and equipment without operator and of personal and household goods	Consumer price index	IC
711. 712.	Renting of transport equipment; renting of other machinery and equipment	Consumer price index excluding rents	PO
713.	Renting of personal and household goods	Implicit price index for private consumption expenditure (for other services to households)	BE
72. 73. 74.	Computer and related activities; research and development; other business activities	Consumer price index (for services)	BE
72. 73. 74. (exc. 7411)	Computer and related activities; research and development; other business activities	Wage rate index	NE
73. part 74	Research and development; other business activities	Index of average wages and salaries per full time equivalent employees	US

3. EXTRAPOLATION OF VALUE ADDED

71. 72. 73. 74.	Renting of machinery and equipment without operator and of personal and household goods; computer and related activities; research and development; other business activities	Output volume index (consumer price index taken as deflator)	LU
		Index of number of working proprietors and of number of hours paid	NZ

71. 72. 73. 749.	Renting of machinery and equipment without operator and of personal and household goods; computer and related activities; research and development; business activities n.e.c.	Implied volume index for the business services that are separately identified	IR
71. 72. 74.	Renting of machinery and equipment without operator and of personal and household goods; computer related activities; other business activities	Index of hours worked	AL
71. 72. part 74	Renting of machinery and equipment without operator and of personal and household goods; computer related activities; other business activities (excluding advertising)	Volume index based on rate of increase of total employment	SP
711. 712.	Renting of transport equipment; renting of other machinery and equipment	Output physical quantity index based on number of leasing contracts	AU
711.	Renting of transport equipment	Output volume index based on constant price expenditure on self-drive cars	UK
712. 713. 72. 73. part 74	Renting of machinery and equipment; renting of personal and household goods n.e.c.; computer and related activities; other business activities	Weighted employment index using average wages and salaries per full-time equivalent employees	US
712.	Renting of other machinery and equipment	Index of constant price turnover (of hirers of industrial goods)	UK
713.	Renting of personal and household goods	Output volume index of retail sales for relevant activities	UK
		Output volume index (price index of durable and semi-durable goods used as deflator)	AU
72. 73. 74.	Computer and related activities; research and development; other business activities	Index of numbers employed adjusted for labour productivity change	AU

72. 7414. 742. 743. 749.	Computer and related activities; business and management consultancy; architectural, engineering and other technical activities; advertising; business activities n.e.c.	Average of index of man-years worked and output volume index (building cost index used as deflator)	IC
72.	Computer and related activities	Constant price turnover index (weighted combination of specific output prices and wage rates used as deflator	UK
73. part 74 (esc. 7411, 7412)	Research and development; other business activities (excluding legal activities; accounting, bookkeeping and auditing activities; tax consultancy)	Index of numbers employed adjusted for changes in labour productivity	UK
73.	Research and development	Index of numbers employed	SP, NZ
		Quarterly number of hours worked is benchmarked to annual index of final consumption expenditure on research and development	AL
74.	Other business activities	Deflated wage bill index (consumer price index used as deflator)	SW
		Output volume index to which the ratio of value added to output is applied	TU
74.(excl 7411, 7412)	Other business activities (excluding legal activities; accounting, bookkeeping and auditing activities; tax consultancy)	Index of numbers employed adjusted for labour productivity change	UK
74. (exc. 749)	Other business activities (excl. business activities n.e.c.)	Index of numbers employed	IR
7411. 7412. 7413.	Legal activities; bookkeeping, auditing and tax consultancy; market research and public opinion polling	Index of number of man-years worked	IC
7411.	Legal activities	Physical quantity output index (number of mortgage advances) and index of number of court proceedings employees, adjusted for productivity change	UK

| 7412. | Accounting, bookkeeping, and auditing activities, tax consultancy | Turnover volume index (current price turnover deflated by average earnings for non manual services) | UK |

4. OTHER METHOD:

CONTROLLED DOUBLE DEFLATION OR EXTRAPOLATION/DEFLATION

(A preliminary estimate of constant price value added is obtained as a residual between constant price gross output and calculated intermediate consumption assuming fixed input coefficients in constant prices. Intermediate consumption is then adjusted in an input/output system so that supply equals demand for all service commodity groups. Constant price gross output is obtained either by deflation or extrapolation, as described in column 3)

712. 713.	Renting of other machinery; renting of personal and household goods	Price index used to deflate gross output	SE
72. 74.	Computer and related activities; other business activities	Wage rate index used to deflate gross output	SE
711.	Renting of transport equipment	Physical quantity output index (stock of cars for leasing) used to extrapolate gross output	SE
73.	Research and development	Index of hours worked used to extrapolate gross output	SE

M. Education

1. DOUBLE DEFLATION

80. inc. 923	Education; library archives, museums and other cultural activities	Composite index of implicit price indices of private consumption expenditure for private education, museums, libraries and private education housing and meals	US
		Implicit price index based on university enrollment and constant price output indicator and consumer price index of private lessons	CA
80.	Education	Special estimated price index obtained from price indices of intermediate consumption goods and wage indices of these industries	GE
		Consumer price index (relevant components)	FR, IT
		Net price index of driving schools and music lessons	DE
		Combined consumer price index of education fees and wage price index	NO
809.	Adult and other education	Input cost index	JA

2. EXTRAPOLATION/DEFLATION

| 809. | Adult and other education | Number of driving licenses index used as extrapolator for gross output | FI |

3. DEFLATION OF VALUE ADDED

80.	Education	Implicit private consumption price index (of other services to households)	BE
809.	Adult and other education	Consumer price index (relevant components)	AU
		Consumer price index (for tuition fees)	SP

4. EXTRAPOLATION OF VALUE ADDED

80.	Education	Index of numbers employed adjusted for labour productivity change	UK
		Implied volume index for public education	IR
		Index of numbers employed	LU
		Quarterly number of hours worked benchmarked to annual index of final consumption expenditure on education	AL
		Index of number of students multiplied by number of weeks of teaching	NZ
801. 802. 803.	Primary education; secondary education; higher education	Physical quantity output index based on number of pupils and students	SP

5. OTHER METHOD:

A. CONTROLLED DOUBLE DEFLATION or EXTRAPOLATION/DEFLATION

(A preliminary estimate of constant price value added is obtained as a residual between constant price gross output and calculated intermediate consumption assuming fixed input coefficients in constant prices. Intermediate consumption is then adjusted in an input/output system so that supply equals demand for all service commodity groups. Constant price gross output is obtained either by deflation or extrapolation, as described in column 3)

| part 80 | Education (except driving schools) | Wage rate index used to deflate gross output | SE |
| | Driving schools | Output physical quantity index based on number of licensed pupils used to extrapolate gross output | SE |

B. PART DOUBLE DEFLATION/PART DIRECT DEFLATION

| 809. | Adult and other education | Consumer price index and wage rate index | NE |

N. **Health and social work**

1. DOUBLE DEFLATION

851. 852.	Human health activities; veterinary activities	Consumer price index (relevant components)	FR, IT, SP
851.	Human health activities	Consumer price index (for medical services)	JA
		Special price index based on consumer price statistics (for hospitals), rates of payment per kind of service (for doctors and dentists under compulsoty insurance schemes), special price index based on consumer price statistics (for doctors and dentists under private insurances)	GE
		Net price index for doctors and dental services adjusted for changes in government payment share, net price index for massage, wage index for skilled wage earners for orthopaedists	DE
		Health service price index	FI
part 851 part 853	Human health activities; social work activities	Weighted combination of consumer price index components (for dentists and health care and special care facilities), rates of remuneration of physicians and income price index	CA
part 851	Hospital activities	Composite index of input prices and consumer price index of hospital rooms	US
		Implicit price index (based on dividing labour income by employment)	CA
	Medical and dental practice activities; other human health activities	Consumer price index for physicians, dentists, other professional medical services, out-patient care facilities; composite index of input prices for nursing and personal care	US
	Medical and dental practice activities	Consumer price index for medical services	BE
		Consumer price index (relevant components)	NE
852.	Veterinary activities	Composite price index of agricultural services	US
		Corporate service price index (for veterinary services)	JA
		Special price index based on consumer price statistics	GE

98

		Index of expenditure per hectare in agriculture adjusted for number of animals per hectare in agriculture, average wage index for skilled wage earners and net consumer price index for dog food	DE
		Consumer price index	NE
		Unit price index of consultations	NO

2. EXTRAPOLATION/DEFLATION

851.	Human health activities	Consumer price index (relevant components)	AU

3. DEFLATION OF VALUE ADDED

851.	Human health activities	Consumer price index (relevant components)	AU
part 851	Hospital activities	Implicit private consumption price index for other services to households	BE
		Intermediate consumption price index and index of gross wages per person employed	NE
852.	Veterinary activities	Consumer price index	BE

4. EXTRAPOLATION OF VALUE ADDED

851. 852.	Human health activities; veterinary activities	Index of numbers employed adjusted for labour productivity change	UK
		Index of numbers employed	IR
		Output volume index (consumer price index for medical services and hospital used as deflator)	LU
		Wage bill index deflated by consumer price index for health services	SW
851.	Human health activities	Quarterly number of hours worked benchmarked to annual index of final consumption expenditure on health	AL
		Composite index based on output volume index (measured by constant price government subsidy to medical practitioners), physical quantity index of number of occupied beds and of number of specialists, and index of hours worked	NZ
part 851	Other human health activities	Private consumption volume index of these services	BE

852.	Veterinary activities	Index number of vets adjusted for labour productivity change	AU
		Gross output volume index	FI
		Index of number of registered vets	NZ
853.	Social work activities	Composite physical quantity index based on number employed, numbers in care and number of beds	NZ

5. OTHER METHOD:

A. CONTROLLED DOUBLE DEFLATION or EXTRAPOLATION/DEFLATION

(A preliminary estimate of constant price value added is obtained as a residual between constant price gross output and calculated intermediate consumption assuming fixed input coefficients in constant prices. Intermediate consumption is then adjusted in an input/output system so that supply equals demand for all service commodity groups. Constant price gross output is obtained either by deflation or extrapolation, as described in column 3)

| part 851 | Private medical treatment | Physical quantity index based on number of visits to private doctors used to extrapolate gross output | SE |
| | Dental services | Consumer price index for dental treatment used to deflate gross output | SE |

B. PART DEFLATION, PART EXTRAPOLATION OF VALUE ADDED

| 851. | Human health activities | Consumer price index (relevant components) and index of average man-years worked | IC |

C. PART DEFLATION, PART EXTRAPOLATION OF GROSS OUTPUT

| 851. | Human health activities | Price index of government fees for health services (for hospitals); index of number of doctors and dentists (for medical and dentist services) | NO |

D. BENCHMARK ESTIMATES ASSUMED UNCHANGED

| 852. | Veterinary activities | Base year value remains unchanged in constant prices (volume index = 100) | SE |

O. Other community, social and personal service activities

1. DOUBLE DEFLATION

90. 9211. 922. 93.	Sewage and refuse disposal, sanitation and similar activities; motion picture and video production and distribution; news agency activities; other service activities	Producer price index	FR
90. 922.	Sewage and refuse disposal, sanitation and similar activities; news agency activities	Input cost index	JA
90.	Sewage and refuse disposal, sanitation and similar activities	Consumer price index (relevant components)	US
		Special price index obtained from intermediate consumption price indices and wage indices for this industry	GE
		Combination of wage index, index of tariffs for removal of household garbage, and net price index for chimney and window cleaning	DE
		Composite price index of wage index for cleaning services and price index of waste management	FI
		Wage price index	NO
92.	Recreational, cultural and sporting activities	Consumer price index (relevant components)	IT, SP
92. (exc. 9213 922) 93.	Recreational, cultural and sporting activities; other service activities	Consumer price index (for admission fees, compact discs, lessons, repairs, maintenance, tailoring)	JA
92. (exc. 9212 9213)	Recreational, cultural and sporting activities	Special estimated price index obtained from price indices of intermediate consumption goods and wage indices of these industries	GE
92. (exc. 9211 922)	Recreational, cultural and sporting activities	Consumer price index	FR
9211. 9212.	Motion picture and video production and distribution; motion picture projection	Tax adjusted consumer price index	CA

9211.	Motion picture and video production and distribution	Wage index for unskilled female wage earners	DE
9212.	Motion picture projection	Price index of entrance fee	GE
		Net consumer price index of entrance fee	DE
9212. 9213. 93.	Motion picture projection; radio and television activities; other service activities	Consumer price index (relevant components)	NE
9213.	Radio and television activities	Composite index of advertising cost indices by type of media	US
		Weighted price index of fees and advertising spots	GE
		Cost index of advertising for television	CA
		Radio and TV license adjusted for broadcasting hours	DE
		Combination of TV license price index and programme time price index	FI
		Consumer price index (for radio and TV licenses)	NO
9214. 9219. 9233. part 9241 part 9249	Dramatic arts, music and other arts activities; other entertainment activities; botanical and zoological gardens and nature reserves; sporting activities; other recreational activities	Weighted price index including consumer price index for live shows, spectator sports, CPI all items and for meals	CA
9214. 9219.	Dramatic arts, music and other arts activities; other entertainment activities;	Implicit price index for theatres (output volume based on number of hours played), consumer price index for artist, weighted index of wage indices (orchestras, recording studios, ticket agencies), of wholesale price index for recording tape and net price index for cinemas	DE
part 9214 9219. 924.	Dramatic arts, music and other arts activities; other entertainment activities n.e.c.; sporting and other recreational activities	Consumer price index and implicit price index of private consumption expenditure (for parimutual net receipts)	US

part 9241 part 9249	Sporting activities; other recreational activities	Weighted price index for lotteries and parimutual betting based on consumer price index, all items	CA
923.	Library, archives, museums and other recreational activities	Net price index	DE
924.	Sporting and other recreational activities	Weighted index of net price indices and wage indices; index of average entrance fee (for race courses)	DE
		Wage rate index	NE
93.	Other service activities	Special consumer price indices	GE
		Tax adjusted consumer price index for laundries and other personal services	CA
		Net price index for laundries and hairdressing, implicit price index for funeral services (volume index based on number of deaths), wage index of unskilled male wage-earners for other service activities n.e.c.	DE
		Consumer price index (for betting and lotteries)	SP
part 93	Other service activities	Consumer price index (relevant components)	US

2. DOUBLE EXTRAPOLATION

part 921. 923.	Cinemas, theatres; library, archives, museums and other cultural activities	Physical quantity output index based on number of visitors	NO
part 9214 part 924	Concerts; sporting and other recreational activities	Index of man-hours worked	NO
part 924	Betting and lotteries	Unit price index for betting and lotteries	NO

3. DEFLATION OF VALUE ADDED

90. 9213. 9214. 9219. 924. 93.	Sewage and refuse disposal; sanitation and similar activities; radio and television activities, dramatic arts, music and other arts activities, other entertainment activities n.e.c.; sporting and other recreational activities; other service activities	Consumer price index (relevant components)	AU
90. part 92 93.	Sewage and refuse disposal, sanitation and similar activities; recreational, cultural and sporting activities; other service activities	Consumer price index	LU
90.	Sewage and refuse disposal, sanitation and similar activities	Consumer price index (for other services to enterprises)	BE
		Wage rate index and intermediate consumption price index	NE
921. 923. 924. 93.	Motion picture, radio, television and other entertainment activities; library, archives, museums and other cultural activities; sporting and other recreational activities; other service activities	Implicit price index of private consumption (of other services to households)	BE
9211. 9212. 923.	Motion picture and video production and distribution; motion picture projection; library, archives, museums and other cultural activities	Index of average wages and salaries per full time equivalent employee	US
9212.	Motion picture projection	Consumer price index (relevant components)	IC, LU
922.	News agency activities	Consumer price index for services	BE
		Wage rate index	NE

4. EXTRAPOLATION OF VALUE ADDED

90. 92. (exc. 9213 9219) 93.	Sewage and refuse disposal, sanitation and similar activities; recreational, cultural and sporting activities; other service activities	Output volume index (relevant components of producer price index used as deflators)	NZ

90.	Sewage and refuse disposal, sanitation and similar activities	Index of numbers employed adjusted for labour productivity change	UK
		Implied volume index for identified other business services	IR
		Output volume index based on growth rates of total employment	SP
		Output physical quantity index based on number of premises with sewerage connections	AL
911.	Activities of business, employers and professional organisations	Index of number of members	NZ
921. (exc. 9213) 923. 924.	Motion picture and other entertainment activities; library, archives, museums and other cultural activities; sporting and other recreational activities	Index of numbers employed	NE
921. (exc. 9213 9219) 924.	Motion picture, radio, television and other entertainment activities; sporting and other recreational activities	Output volume index based on constant price private final consumption expenditure on non-gambling entertainment	AL
9211. 9212. 9213.	Motion picture and video production and distribution; motion picture projection; radio and television activities	Output volume index (current price turnover deflated by specific consumer price index)	UK
9211.	Motion picture and video production and distribution	Index of numbers employed	AU
		Output volume index	FI
9212.	Motion picture projection	Output volume index (consumer price index used as deflator) and number of visitors	AU
		Physical quantity index based on number of entrances in cinemas	FI
		Volume index of personal consumer expenditure on cinemas (the consumer price index component for cinemas is used as deflator)	IR
9213.	Radio and television activities	Physical quantity weighted average index of radio and TV hours	IR
		Output volume index based on constant price revenue earned by radio and TV broadcasters	AL

		Output physical quantity index based on number of licensed televisions and on number of hours of local TV content broadcast	NZ
9219. 923. 924. 93.	Other entertainment activities; library, archives, museums and other cultural activities; sporting and other recreational activities; other service activities	Volume indices of components of personal expenditure deflated by appropriate components of consumer price index. Residual parts extrapolated using volume index for separately identified components	IR
9214. 9219. 924.	Dramatic arts, music and other arts activities; other entertainment activities; sporting and other recreational activities	Output volume index (current price turnover deflated by specific consumer price index or deflated expenditure on sport and entertainment) and output physical quantity index based on number of gaming machines	UK
9220. part 93	News agency activities; other service activities	Weighted employment index	US
922.	News agency activities	Implied volume index of identified business services	IR
9219. 924.	Other entertainment activities n.e.c.; sporting and other recreational activities	Physical quantity index based on numbers of visitors	FI
9214.	Dramatic arts, music and other arts activities	Volume index of personal expenditure deflated by relevant part of consumer price index (for theatres); index of numbers employed (for reminder)	IR
9219.	Other entertainment activities	Output volume index based on constant price private final consumption expenditure on gambling	AL
		Output physical quantity index based on number of betting tickets issued and number of lotteries	NZ
93.	Other service activities	Output volume index (turnover deflated by specific consumer price index for laundering and dry-cleaning), deflated expenditure on hairdressing and index number of employees in personal services	UK
		Output volume index	FI

106

		Physical quantity output index based on number of deaths (for funeral services), on population number (for dry-cleaning), output volume index based on constant price turnover using appropriate consumer price index (for hairdressing) and number of hours worked (for other services)	AL

5. OTHER METHOD

A. CONTROLLED DOUBLE DEFLATION or EXTRAPOLATION/DEFLATION

(A preliminary estimate of constant price value added is obtained as a residual between constant price gross output and calculated intermediate consumption assuming fixed input coefficients in constant prices. Intermediate consumption is then adjusted in an input/output system so that supply equals demand for all service commodity groups. Constant price gross output is obtained either by deflation or extrapolation, as described in column 3)

90.	Sewage and refuse disposal, sanitation and similar activities	Wage rate index of salaried employees in manufacturing used to deflate gross output	SE
921. (exc. 9213) part 93	Motion picture and other entertainment activities; other service activities (excluding funeral services)	Consumer price index for recreational activities and other service activities used to deflate gross output	SE
9213.	Radio and television activities	Physical quantity index based on number of TV licenses used to extrapolate gross output	SE
part 93	Funeral services	Physical quantity index based on number of deaths used to extrapolate gross output	SE

B. PART DEFLATION, PART EXTRAPOLATION OF VALUE ADDED

921. (exc. 9211 9212) 93.	Radio, television and other entertainment activities; other service activities	Consumer price index (relevant components) used as deflator and average man-years worked used as extrapolator	IC
924.	Sporting and other recreational activities	Approximate net price index of expenditure used as deflator and index of average man-years worked used as extrapolator	IC

ISIC CODE	ITEM HEADING	DESCRIPTION OF INDEX	COUNTRY
	1. <u>DOUBLE DEFLATION</u>		
(exc. part 91 95)	All non-market services (except business assosiations and labour organisations and private households with employed persons)	Implicit hourly wage price index (by purpose of government consumption expenditure) for wages; implicit price index of gross fixed capital formation for capital consumption; implicit price index for other taxes linked to production (constant price taxes are held equal to their base year value)	DE
75. 80. 85. 73. 90 91. 923. 924.	Public administration and defence; compulsory social security; education; health and social work; research and development; sewage and refuse disposal, sanitation and similar activities; activities of membership organisations n.e.c.; library, archives, museums and other cultural activities; sporting and other recreational activities	Implicit output deflator based on an input cost index calculated as sum of deflated intermediate consumption, compensation of employees, fixed capital consumption and indirect taxes	JA
75.	Public administration and defence; compulsory social security	Combined price index for consumption of fixed capital and compensation of employees	NO
80. 73. 851.	Education; research and development; human health activities	Combined input price index for producers of government services	NO
part 91 95	Activities of membership organisations n.e.c.; private households with employed persons	Wage index for salary earners in business associations and labour organisations; wage index of domestic staff	DE
921. 95.	Motion picture, radio, television and other entertainment activities; private households with employed persons	Consumer price index (for TV license fee and for domestic help)	JA
part 851 9213. 93.	Radio and television activities; other service activities	Consumer price index (relevant components)	NE
95.	Private households with employed persons	Consumer price index (for domestic help services)	IT

2. DOUBLE EXTRAPOLATION

853. 91. 92.	Social work activities; activities of membership organisations; recreational, cultural and sporting activities	Index of man-hours worked	NO

3. EXTRAPOLATION/DEFLATION

75. 73.	Public administration and defence; compulsory social security; research and development	Index of number of employees (for general public services, foreign affairs, research, recreational activities, exonomic and housing policy administration); index of number of court proceedings (for judicial activities); index of number of employees and resident population (for defence); index of number of employees and of acts performed (for social security); number of inpatients in hospitals and homes for the aged and number of children in creches and orphanages (for social work activities)	IT
80.	Education	Index of number of teachers and pupils by type of course divided by average number of pupils per class (the latter being taken as an indicator for quality)	IT
8511.	Hospital activities	Synthetic index obtained by dividing the average index of number of employees and of inpatients by the average length of hospitalisation (the latter being taken as an indicator of quality)	IT
8512. 8519.	Medical and dental practice activities; other human health activities	Index of numbers employed	IT
853.	Social work activities	Index of four monthly moving average of number of employees	IT

4. DEFLATION OF VALUE ADDED

	All non-market services	Wage rate index for compensation of employees and constant price fixed capital consumption	IC
(exc. 95)	All non-market services except private households	Wage rate index for compensation of employees and constant price fixed capital consumption calculated in a capital stock model	FI

75. 80. 73. 851. 852. 853. 90. 92.	Public administration and defence; compulsory social security; education; research and development; veterinary activities; social work activities (govern-ment operated), sewage and refuse disposal, sanitation and similar activities (government operated); recreational, cultural and sporting activities (government operated)	Wage rate index (compensation of employees deflated by wage indices of special groups of employees) adjusted for labour productivity change and for depreciation	GE
75. 80. 73. 853. 90. 92.	Public administration and defence; compulsory social security; education; research and development; social work activities; sewage and refuse disposal, sanitation and similar activities; recreational, cultural and sporting activities	Wage rate index	BE
75. (exc. 7522/3 853. 90 911.	Public administration and defence; compulsory social security; social work activities; sewage and refuse disposal, sanitation and similar activities; activities of business, employers and professional organisations	Standard wage index for government employees	AU
75. 73. 80.	Public administration and defence; compulsory social security; education; research and development	Wage rate index and constant price capital consumption price index (implicit price index of capital stock used as deflator) adjusted for labour productivity change	NE
75. 73. 90.	Public administration and defence; compulsory social security; research and development; sewage and refuse disposal, sanitation and similar activities	Wage index of civil servants Public service wage index	FR IR
part 7513 part 9214 part 924	Regulation of and contribution to more efficient operation of business; dramatic arts, music and other arts activities; sporting and other recreational activities	Average weekly earnings index (for salaries and wages and supplementary labour income), implicit price index of capital stock (for capital consumption)	CA

75.	Public administration and defence; compulsory social security	Public sector wage rate index	PO
part 75	Public administration and defence; compulsory social security	Wage rate index of all industries	NZ
851. 853. 73. 91. 923. 924.	Human health activities; social work activities; research and development; activities of membership organisations n.e.c.; library, archives, museums and other cultural activities; sporting and other recreational activities; (operated by non-government/ non-profit institutions)	Index of average wages and salaries per full time equivalent employee	US
8512.	Medical and dental practice activities	Consumer price index of dental and health care, index of rates of remuneration of physicians under provincial health plans, capital consumption price index (implicit price index of capital stock used as deflator)	CA
part 851	Human health activities	Index of gross wages per person employed	NE
8519. part 853 part 91	Other human health activities; social work activities; activities of membership organisations n.e.c.	Wage rate index based on provincial and municipal wages and implicit price index of capital stock used as deflator for capital consumption	CA
853. 91. (exc. 911) 92.	Social work activities; activities of membership organisations n.e.c.; recreational, cultural and sporting activities	Wage index	FR
853.	Social work activities; activities of membership organisations n.e.c.	Wage rate index for all industries	NZ
part 853 part 91	Social work activities; activities of membership organisations n.e.c.	Wage price index partly based on employment index partly based on index of average weekly earnings and implicit price index of capital stock used as deflator for capital consumption	CA
90. 91.	Sewage and refuse disposal, sanitation and similar activities; activities of membership organisations	Wage rate index	NE

91. (exc. 911)	Activities of membership organisations n.e.c.	Wage price index based on weekly earnings (trade unions and religious organisations), consumer price index of service commodities (political parties) and implicit price index of capital stock used as deflator for capital consumption	CA
		Wage rate index of salaried employees in manufacturing	SE
911.	Activities of business, employers and professional organisations	Consumer price index for services	BE
912. 919.	Activities of trade unions, activities of other membership organisations	Private consumption implicit price index	BE
92.	Recreational, cultural and sporting activities	Standard wage index and consumer price index	AU
95.	Private households with employed persons	Gross output price index	US
		Consumer price index	NE
			FR
		Hourly wage rate	CA
		Weighted consumer price index for domestic services, childcare in the house and outside the home	

5. EXTRAPOLATION OF VALUE ADDED

(exc. 95)	All non-market services	Index of numbers employed adjusted for labour productivity (+0.5 %)	LU
	All non-market services (except private households with employed persons)	Output volume index (consumer price index for services used to deflate output)	SW
(exc. 91 95)	All non-market services (except activities of membership organisations and private households with employed persons)	Deflated compensation of employees index (using an index of number of hours worked as extrapolator) and index of constant price fixed capital consumption (calculated directly from constant price capital stock estimated)	SE

75. 6411. 73. 85. 90. 921. 923. 924.	Public administration and defence; compulsory social security; national post; research and development (government operated); health and social work (government operated; sewage and refuse disposal, sanitation and similar activities; motion picture, radio, tele-vision and other entertainment activities; library, archives, museums and other cultural activities; sporting and other recreational activities (government operated)	Index of numbers employed (federal, defence: full time equivalent employment by rank and length of service; federal, non-defence: full time equivalent employment by grade, adjusted for change in hours worked; state and local non-education and education: full time equivalent employment adjusted for change from base year in hours worked)	US
75.	Public administration and defence; compulsory social security	Combination of constant price wage bill index (for the armed forces) and index of numbers employed by grade and activity and constant price non trading capital consumption index	UK
part 75	Public administration and devence; compulsory social security (General government)	Weighted index of numbers employed (using base year compensation of employees in each government department as weights)	NZ
	(Local government)	Deflated wage bill index (producer price index of local government services used as deflator)	NZ
751. 7521. 7522.	Administration of the State and the economic and social policy of the community; foreign affairs; defence activities	Index of hours worked	AL
7522. 7523. 73. 851. 852. 95.	Defence activities; public order and safety activities; research and development; human health activities; veterinary activities; private households with employed persons	Index of numbers employed	AU
7522.	Defence activities	Weighted index of numbers employed by rank (base year salaries and wages used as weights)	CA
part 7523	Public order and safety (Fire Service Commission)	Index of number of permanent employees	NZ
part 753	Compulsory social security activities (Accident Compensation Corporation)	Output physical quantity index based on number of claims	NZ

73. 80. 85. 91. 92. 95.	Research and development, education, health and social work; recreational, cultural and sporting activities (operated by private non-profit institutions serving households); private households with employed persons	Index of numbers employed	GE
73. 80. 90. 91.	Research and development; education; health; sewage and refuse disposal; activities of membership organisations n.e.c.	Deflated wage bill index and numbers employed	PO
80. 851.	Education; human health activities	Physical quantity index	FR
80.	Education	Combination of index of numbers of teachers and constant price non trading capital consumption index	UK
		Weighted average volume index of pupil and teachers numbers	IR
		Index of pupil-weeks taught in different types of institutions	NZ
801. 802. 803. 809.	Primary education; secondary education; higher education; adult and other education	Index of number of teachers	AU
		Output volume index (consumer price index used as output deflator)	AU
851. 852.	Human health activities; veterinary activities	Constant price wage index of National Health Service employees, index of number of general practitioners, output volume index of dentists and constant price NHS non trading capital consumption	UK
851.	Human health activities	Weighted physical quantity output index based on number of beds and number of outpatient treatments (weights derived from base year expenditure on each health service provided)	NZ
		Index of numbers employed	IR
853. 90. 92.	Social work activities; sewage and refuse disposal, sanitation and similar activities; recreational, cultural and sporting activities	Combination of index of number of local authority employees and constant price local authority capital consumption index	UK

853, 92 (exc. 922 and 9213).	Social work activities; recreational, cultural and sporting activities	Index of numbers employed	NE
853.	Social work activities	Index of personal expenditure on charitable and welfare services deflated by overall consumer price index	IR
91. 92.	Activities of membership organisations n.e.c.; recreational, cultural and sporting activities	Index of average wage per employee and index of numbers employed	SP
91.	Activities of membership organisation	Index of numbers employed	IT
912. 919.	Activities of trade unions; activities of other membership organisations	Index of number of members	AU
92.	Recreational, cultural and sporting activities	Index of numbers employed in libraries	PO
95.	Private households with employed persons	Index of constant price expenditure on domestic services	UK
		Index of numbers employed	BE, FI, LU, SE
		Index of full time equivalent employees based on man-years	IC
		Volume index of personal expenditure deflated by consumer price index	IR
		Index of total employment and average wage index	SP
		Index of deflated wage bill (consumer price index for these activities used as deflator)	SW
		Index of general population level	NZ

6. OTHER METHOD:

PART DEFLATION, PART EXTRAPOLATION OF VALUE ADDED

75. 80. 851. 853. 90.	Public administration and defence; compulsory social security; education, human health activities; social work activities; sewage and refuse disposal, sanitation and similar activities	Index of deflated wage bill per employee (used to extrapolate compensation of employees) and price index of gross capital formation of government used to deflate capital consumption	SP

116

75. (exc. part 7513 7522)	Public administration; compulsory social security	Index of numbers employed to extrapolate base year labour income for federal and provincial government operated services, index of average weekly earnings to deflate labour income for municipal government and implicit price index of capital stock to deflate capital consumption	CA
part 7513	Regulation of and contribution to more efficient operation of business	Index of numbers employed (for federal and provincial government operated services), index of average weekly hours (for municipal government) and implicit price index of capital stock used to deflate capital consumption	CA
801. 802.	Primary education; secondary education	Index of number of full time teachers used to extrapolate labour income and implicit price index of capital stock used to deflate capital consumption	CA
803. 809.	Higher education; adult and other education	Output volume index based on enrollment and implicit price index of capital stock used to deflate capital consumption	CA
8511. 921. (exc. 9214)	Hospital activities; motion picture, radio, television and other entertainment activities	Index of numbers employed used to extrapolate labour income and implicit price index of capital stock used to deflate capital consumption	CA

Categories	Group	Class	Description
G			WHOLESALE AND RETAIL TRADE; REPAIR OF MOTOR VEHICLES, MOTORCYCLES AND PERSONAL AND HOUSE-HOLD GOODS
	Division 50		Sale, maintenance and repair of motor vehicles and motorcycles; retail sale of automotive fuel
	Division 51		Wholesale trade and commission trade, except of motor vehicles and motorcycles
	Division 52		Retail trade, except of motor vehicles and motorcycles; repair of personal and household goods
H			HOTELS AND RESTAURANTS
	Division 55		Hotels and restaurants
	551	5510	*Hotels; camping sites and other provision of short-stay accomodation*
	552	5520	*Restaurants, bars and canteens*
I			TRANSPORT, STORAGE AND COMMUNICATIONS
	Division 60		Land transport; transport via pipelines
	601	6010	*Transport via railways*
	602		Other land transport
	603	6030	*Transport via pipelines*
	Division 61		Water transport
	611	6110	*See and coastal water transport*
	612	6120	*Inland water transport*
	Division 62		Air transport
	Division 63		Supporting and auxiliary transport activities: activities of travel agencies
	Division 64		Post and Telecommunications
	641		Post and courier activities
	642	6420	*Telecommunications*

J		FINANCIAL INTERMEDIATION
	Division 65	Financial intermediation, except insurance and pension funding
	651	Monetary intermediation
	659	Other financial intermediation
	Division 66	Insurance and pension funding, except compulsory social security
	6601	*Life insurance*
	6602	*Pension funding*
	6603	*Non-life insurance*
	Division 67	Activitise auxiliary to financial intermediation
K		REAL ESTATE, RENTING AND BUSINESS ACTIVITIES
	Division 70	Real estate activities
	Division 71	Renting of machinery and equipment without operator and of personal and household goods
	711	Renting of transport equipment
	712	Renting of other machinery and equipment
	713 7130	*Renting of personal and household goods n.e.c.*
	Division 72	Computer and related activities
	Division 73	Research and development
	Division 74	Other business activities
	7411	*Legal activities*
	7412	*Accounting, book-keeping and auditing activities: tax consultancy*
	7413	*Market research and public opinion polling*
	7414	*Business and management consultancy activities*
	742	Architectural, engineering and other technical activities
	743 7430	*Advertising*
	749	Business activities n.e.c.
L		PUBLIC ADMINISTRATION AND DEFENCE: COMPULSORY SOCIAL SECURITY
	Division 75	Public administration and defence; compulsory social security
	751	Administration of the State and the economic and social policy of the community

	7511	*General (overall) public service activities*
	7512	*Regulation of the activities of agencies that provide health care, education, cultural services and other social services, excluding social security*
	7513	*Regulation of and contribution to more efficient operation of business*
	7514	*Ancillary service activities for the Government as a whole*
752		Provision of services to the communicy as a whole
	7521	*Foreign affairs*
	7522	*Defence activities*
	7523	*Public order and safety activities*
753	7530	*Compulsory social security activities*

M   EDUCATION

Division 80   Education

801	8010	*Primary education*
802		Secondary education
803	8030	*Higher education*
809	8090	*Adult and other education*

N   HEALTH AND SOCIAL WORK

851		Human health activities
852	8520	Veterinary activities
853		Social work activities

O   OTHER COMMUNITY, SOCIAL AND PERSONAL SERVICE ACTIVITIES

Division 90   Sewage and refuse disposal, sanitation and similar activities

Division 91   Activities of membership organisations n.e.c.

911   Activities of business, employers and professional organisations

| 912 | 9120 | *Activities of trade unions* |

919   Activities of other membership organisations

Division 92   Recreational, cultural and sporting activities

921   Motion picture and video production and distribution

	9211	*Motion picture and video production and distribution*
	9212	*Motion picture projection*
	9213	*Radio and television activities*

	9214	*Dramatic arts, music and other arts activities*
	9219	*Other entertainment activities n.e.c.*
922	9220	*News agency activities*
923		Library, archives, museums and other cultural activities
924		Sporting and other recreational activities
Division 93		Other service activities

P   PRIVATE HOUSEHOLDS WITH EMPLOYED PERSONS

Division 95   Private households with employed persons

Q   EXTRA-TERRITORIAL ORGANISATIONS AND BODIES

Division 99   Extra-territorial organisations and bodies

MAIN SALES OUTLETS OF OECD PUBLICATIONS
PRINCIPAUX POINTS DE VENTE DES PUBLICATIONS DE L'OCDE

ARGENTINA – ARGENTINE
Carlos Hirsch S.R.L.
Galería Güemes, Florida 165, 4° Piso
1333 Buenos Aires   Tel. (1) 331.1787 y 331.2391
Telefax: (1) 331.1787

AUSTRALIA – AUSTRALIE
D.A. Information Services
648 Whitehorse Road, P.O.B 163
Mitcham, Victoria 3132   Tel. (03) 9210.7777
Telefax: (03) 9210.7788

AUSTRIA – AUTRICHE
Gerold & Co.
Graben 31
Wien I   Tel. (0222) 533.50.14
Telefax: (0222) 512.47.31.29

BELGIUM – BELGIQUE
Jean De Lannoy
Avenue du Roi 202 Koningslaan
B-1060 Bruxelles   Tel. (02) 538.51.69/538.08.41
Telefax: (02) 538.08.41

CANADA
Renouf Publishing Company Ltd.
1294 Algoma Road
Ottawa, ON K1B 3W8   Tel. (613) 741.4333
Telefax: (613) 741.5439
Stores:
61 Sparks Street
Ottawa, ON K1P 5R1   Tel. (613) 238.8985
12 Adelaide Street West
Toronto, ON M5H 1L6   Tel. (416) 363.3171
Telefax: (416)363.59.63

Les Éditions La Liberté Inc.
3020 Chemin Sainte-Foy
Sainte-Foy, PQ G1X 3V6   Tel. (418) 658.3763
Telefax: (418) 658.3763

Federal Publications Inc.
165 University Avenue, Suite 701
Toronto, ON M5H 3B8   Tel. (416) 860.1611
Telefax: (416) 860.1608

Les Publications Fédérales
1185 Université
Montréal, QC H3B 3A7   Tel. (514) 954.1633
Telefax: (514) 954.1635

CHINA – CHINE
China National Publications Import
Export Corporation (CNPIEC)
16 Gongti E. Road, Chaoyang District
P.O. Box 88 or 50
Beijing 100704 PR   Tel. (01) 506.6688
Telefax: (01) 506.3101

CHINESE TAIPEI – TAIPEI CHINOIS
Good Faith Worldwide Int'l. Co. Ltd.
9th Floor, No. 118, Sec. 2
Chung Hsiao E. Road
Taipei   Tel. (02) 391.7396/391.7397
Telefax: (02) 394.9176

**CZECH REPUBLIC –
RÉPUBLIQUE TCHÈQUE**
Artia Pegas Press Ltd.
Narodni Trida 25
POB 825
111 21 Praha 1   Tel. (2) 242 246 04
Telefax: (2) 242 278 72

DENMARK – DANEMARK
Munksgaard Book and Subscription Service
35, Nørre Søgade, P.O. Box 2148
DK-1016 København K   Tel. (33) 12.85.70
Telefax: (33) 12.93.87

EGYPT – ÉGYPTE
Middle East Observer
41 Sherif Street
Cairo   Tel. 392.6919
Telefax: 360-6804

FINLAND – FINLANDE
Akateeminen Kirjakauppa
Keskuskatu 1, P.O. Box 128
00100 Helsinki

Subscription Services/Agence d'abonnements :
P.O. Box 23
00371 Helsinki   Tel. (358 0) 121 4416
Telefax: (358 0) 121.4450

FRANCE
OECD/OCDE
Mail Orders/Commandes par correspondance :
2, rue André-Pascal
75775 Paris Cedex 16   Tel. (33-1) 45.24.82.00
Telefax: (33-1) 49.10.42.76
Telex: 640048 OCDE
Internet: Compte.PUBSINQ @ oecd.org
Orders via Minitel, France only/
Commandes par Minitel, France exclusivement :
36 15 OCDE

OECD Bookshop/Librairie de l'OCDE :
33, rue Octave-Feuillet
75016 Paris   Tel. (33-1) 45.24.81.81
(33-1) 45.24.81.67

Dawson
B.P. 40
91121 Palaiseau Cedex   Tel. 69.10.47.00
Telefax : 64.54.83.26

Documentation Française
29, quai Voltaire
75007 Paris   Tel. 40.15.70.00

Economica
49, rue Héricart
75015 Paris   Tel. 45.78.12.92
Telefax : 40.58.15.70

Gibert Jeune (Droit-Économie)
6, place Saint-Michel
75006 Paris   Tel. 43.25.91.19

Librairie du Commerce International
10, avenue d'Iéna
75016 Paris   Tel. 40.73.34.60

Librairie Dunod
Université Paris-Dauphine
Place du Maréchal-de-Lattre-de-Tassigny
75016 Paris   Tel. 44.05.40.13

Librairie Lavoisier
11, rue Lavoisier
75008 Paris   Tel. 42.65.39.95

Librairie des Sciences Politiques
30, rue Saint-Guillaume
75007 Paris   Tel. 45.48.36.02

P.U.F.
49, boulevard Saint-Michel
75005 Paris   Tel. 43.25.83.40

Librairie de l'Université
12a, rue Nazareth
13100 Aix-en-Provence   Tel. (16) 42.26.18.08

Documentation Française
165, rue Garibaldi
69003 Lyon   Tel. (16) 78.63.32.23

Librairie Decitre
29, place Bellecour
69002 Lyon   Tel. (16) 72.40.54.54

Librairie Sauramps
Le Triangle
34967 Montpellier Cedex 2   Tel. (16) 67.58.85.15
Tekefax: (16) 67.58.27.36

A la Sorbonne Actual
23, rue de l'Hôtel-des-Postes
06000 Nice   Tel. (16) 93.13.77.75
Telefax: (16) 93.80.75.69

GERMANY – ALLEMAGNE
OECD Publications and Information Centre
August-Bebel-Allee 6
D-53175 Bonn   Tel. (0228) 959.120
Telefax: (0228) 959.12.17

GREECE – GRÈCE
Librairie Kauffmann
Mavrokordatou 9
106 78 Athens   Tel. (01) 32.55.321
Telefax: (01) 32.30.320

HONG-KONG
Swindon Book Co. Ltd.
Astoria Bldg. 3F
34 Ashley Road, Tsimshatsui
Kowloon, Hong Kong   Tel. 2376.2062
Telefax: 2376.0685

HUNGARY – HONGRIE
Euro Info Service
Margitsziget, Európa Ház
1138 Budapest   Tel. (1) 111.62.16
Telefax: (1) 111.60.61

ICELAND – ISLANDE
Mál Mog Menning
Laugavegi 18, Pósthólf 392
121 Reykjavik   Tel. (1) 552.4240
Telefax: (1) 562.3523

INDIA – INDE
Oxford Book and Stationery Co.
Scindia House
New Delhi 110001   Tel. (11) 331.5896/5308
Telefax: (11) 332.5993
17 Park Street
Calcutta 700016   Tel. 240832

INDONESIA – INDONÉSIE
Pdii-Lipi
P.O. Box 4298
Jakarta 12042   Tel. (21) 573.34.67
Telefax: (21) 573.34.67

IRELAND – IRLANDE
Government Supplies Agency
Publications Section
4/5 Harcourt Road
Dublin 2   Tel. 661.31.11
Telefax: 475.27.60

ISRAEL – ISRAËL
Praedicta
5 Shatner Street
P.O. Box 34030
Jerusalem 91430   Tel. (2) 52.84.90/1/2
Telefax: (2) 52.84.93

R.O.Y. International
P.O. Box 13056
Tel Aviv 61130   Tel. (3) 546 1423
Telefax: (3) 546 1442

Palestinian Authority/Middle East:
INDEX Information Services
P.O.B. 19502
Jerusalem   Tel. (2) 27.12.19
Telefax: (2) 27.16.34

ITALY – ITALIE
Libreria Commissionaria Sansoni
Via Duca di Calabria 1/1
50125 Firenze   Tel. (055) 64.54.15
Telefax: (055) 64.12.57
Via Bartolini 29
20155 Milano   Tel. (02) 36.50.83